VEDA

SPIRITUALITY FOR
LEADERSHIP & SUCCESS

Ultimate Spiritual Lessons,
based on the PowerTalks and MysticTalks of

PRANAY

BEL!EF

Published by

FiNGERPRINT! **BEL!EF**

An imprint of Prakash Books India Pvt. Ltd.

113/A, Darya Ganj, New Delhi-110 002,
Tel: (011) 2324 7062 – 65, Fax: (011) 2324 6975
Email: info@prakashbooks.com/sales@prakashbooks.com

facebook www.facebook.com/fingerprintpublishing
twitter www.twitter.com/FingerprintP
www.fingerprintpublishing.com

ISBN: 978 93 9039 101 1

Processed & printed in India

"O Ram, when the mind is calm it is free!"

Yoga Vasishtha

Preface

Vedanta is the very heart of India's mysticism and spirituality. It contains the most essential principles for life, leadership, and success. This book distils the essence of Vedanta for positive leadership and truly successful living.

These lessons are especially important in a world where leaders, and all those seeking success, have to make tough decisions during crisis situations: pandemics (such as Covid-19), economic instability, and so on.

For thousands of years, the *rishis*/seers, sages, and mystics of India have investigated the basis of human behaviour, the impulses of man and his relationship with the cosmos. Out of these investigations have come about the most important keys for materially and spiritually successful living. And the greatest part is that Vedantic philosophy has great resonance with modern neuroscience, psychology, and modern corporate/management theories. It also is in many ways the basis and foundation of world spiritual paths such as Japanese Zen, which several of the greatest business leaders and leaders of all kinds have looked to for creativity, aesthetic, and inspiration.

Quite simply, Vedanta echoes the best of India's Upanishadic, Vedic, and Hindu wisdom. These core teachings are very useful for leaders, and for all those needing deep inspiration for true success!

Pranay

"There is the Light of lights which is the inner being.
The peerless spirit within living beings . . .
the immortal light"
Yajur Veda

"If inwardly one is cool the whole world will be cool!
If inwardly one is agitated or anxious,
the whole world will look like it is burning!"
Yoga Vasishtha

Contents

CHAPTER-1

Adi Shankaracharya: Mystic Principles for Leaders

LESSON: Adi Shankaracharya gave a clear-cut idea of Vedanta, by speaking of it as the recognition of the divine within you. All of Vedanta's highest teachings begin with this spiritual assertion. For leadership and success, this idea of the divine within becomes a tremendously empowering philosophy. It makes one have the guts and fearlessness to face up to any crisis or difficult situation.

Vedanta—the ancient mystical philosophy of India—is very important for leadership and success as it creates root level mental strength, clarity, decision-making speed/power, execution effectiveness, charisma, and values-based leadership traits.

Vedanta says that to realize our highest capability, the first essential thing is that we know ourselves to be *pure and divine consciousness*. The great guru of Vedanta, Adi Shankaracharya, says, 'All beings are by nature pure consciousness itself. It is due to ignorance that they appear to be different from it.' And the ultimate text on Vedanta, the Yoga Vasishtha, says, 'You are bound on all sides by the idea, "I am the body." Cut that bond by the sword of knowledge "I am consciousness" and be happy!'

So Vedanta is echoing the highest spiritual truth: that knowing yourself as pure consciousness is the essential, mystical key to going past all fears, self-limitations in happiness, and all inhibitions! And of moving *towards* your complete self-actualization and potential-realization. Why is that? Because, when you know yourself to be pure consciousness, you are not afraid anymore! You are not fearful of anything happening to the mind-body complex. You are able to take on all challenges with a great courage in your heart: That is essentially what a dynamic leader's consciousness should be all about. Leaders need to feel full of strength, full of the hopeful feeling and attitude that nothing can hinder us from truly successful living— simply because consciousness cannot ever be hindered by material circumstances.

In the face of very difficult situations—such as global

epidemics and downturns—it is key for us to imbibe and understand this.

When a person inculcates such an attitude, it takes him or her not only towards a more meditative view, a more intuitive view of life, but towards a more fearless view. And that is why Vedanta is so important for leaders to understand. It is fundamentally about developing the calm realization that our innermost consciousness is capable of facing all situations with the power of wisdom, serenity, undisturbed bliss, and dynamism.

The whole message of the Vedas, the Upanishads, the sacred 'Shruti' literature of India and of Sanatan Dharma or Hinduism itself, is that God is pure consciousness and we are an integral part of that consciousness! That is our ultimate reality. Once we know this, we relax into a feeling that we are able to take on anything that comes our way in life! And doing so, we feel that all our anxieties in life have dissolved. So from the success and leadership perspectives, it is imperative that to truly function fearlessly and with a broader vision, we must expand our vista of seeing into the ultimate reality of consciousness. That gives us a far greater vision of things; it allows us to move past the mechanical, to move past the status quo, and to act with great intuition. We are to know that behind the material lies a great wealth of the spiritual. And that spiritual part of ourselves—

which is consciousness—is enough to help us meet all our material goals as well. Evolved leaders who seek to go beyond the ordinary must understand this spiritual principle of consciousness.

Evolution in the way we view ourselves is key to how we act within the world. When a person can view himself/herself as being far greater than body-mind and limiting circumstances, and as part of the entire cosmic consciousness itself, a deeply rooted self-faith and inspirational power are born within the individual. And these traits of rooted self-faith plus inspirational power are what generate great thought and leadership action. Hence, the understanding of consciousness is the master key for dynamic leaders.

We must understand a few things about the cosmic or universal aspect of our reality also. Now, before Albert Einstein, the view of the cosmos was that it is mechanical. Einstein went past the mechanical understanding of the world and realized that behind the mechanical view of existence lies the subtle realm of energy. According to Vedanta, beyond universal energy also is the ultimate consciousness! This supreme consciousness is the procreator of all things. Through Vedantists such as Swami Vivekananda and others, there has arisen an understanding that we are composed of something truly profound: the same pure consciousness that brings forth the whole universe. It is very important for us to identify ourselves as beings of pure consciousness, especially for leaders: because they have a special role in guiding others. In the modern age, great scientists such as Dr. George Sudarshan (who's been nominated so many times for the Nobel Prize in physics) are also saying that the Upanishads and Vedas have told us about the singularity of life as a product of a mysterious higher consciousness-energy. This singularity of unlimited consciousness-energy is what all things are, but we human beings often mistake ourselves to be limited in scope. That is the most destructive aspect when it comes to our mentality and view of ourselves. Know yourself to be infinite in consciousness, says Vedanta, and then you will succeed in living a higher quality of life. This is very, very important for leaders to understand: it gives self-confidence and enables them to give hope and real confidence to others too. Great leaders inspire true confidence.

When you know yourself to be pure consciousness, what can distress you? Nothing can, because you are able to go past the limited material view of self and others. And through this understanding, you come to know that at your roots, you are actually beyond all anxiety, fear, frustration. This is what Krishna's Bhagavad Gita is all about. Krishna is telling Arjun, again and again on the battlefield in the Mahabharat, that knowing himself as pure consciousness, knowing himself as pure soul or *atma* is the very secret. Because then only can you feel peace within yourself. By identifying with your mind-body complex, you're never at peace with yourself, because you're always anxious about circumstances and about what the results will be.

The mystic sciences of both Vedanta and Raja Yoga of India say that the most essential thing is to feel your spiritual power, and that is the power of consciousness. Through that, your mind-power and your physical-material powers expand into a great freedom of being, because of which you start acting with dynamism! And dynamism in action is really what a good leader should be demonstrating in his or her own life.

Therefore, through understanding this primary principle of consciousness, Adi Shankara is giving us a clear way to fulfil our higher potential—as individuals and as leaders in whatever leadership position we are in life. And remember, Vedanta is not about a particular religion as such. It is about realizing our ultimate state of being, which is achieved in the state of pure freedom of perception: in other words, of moving towards enlightenment/*mukti*/*moksha*/nirvana/*samadhi*, towards what has been called *satori* in Zen philosophy. It's all about finding the echo of the divine consciousness within your very heartbeat and within the very core of your mind. For then you find yourself becoming intense, more rooted and established in whatever you do. Because now, all fear vanishes: fear about what will happen to your body-mind complex and so on. Through consciousness realization, you transcend the physical level. You suddenly feel completely empowered and relaxed. You begin trusting your own self-power much more. And through that, the leader comes to a greater purity of energy, a greater release of one's higher energy into whatever one has been doing.

Our most limiting factor in life is psychological fear. To go beyond psychological fear, the Vedantic prescription is very simple: simply understand yourself mystically as being composed of pure consciousness. Then your thoughts and actions become integrated. You find great courage, you find great strength, and you find the ability to flower to your utmost potential! Consciousness is the bedrock of your being—know yourself as being comprised of this supreme consciousness within the very foundation of yourselves. Then you move towards successful living in all aspects of life. Plus, you're able to take others towards more successful lives. And a leader who can do that, is a truly great leader.

The second principle Adi Shankaracharya talks about is regarding the nature of mind. He explains that supreme consciousness exists beyond the individual mind. He says, 'There is no ignorance outside the mind. The mind alone is ignorance or *avidya*, the cause of bondage! When that is destroyed, all else is destroyed!' In other words, what Adi Shankara is saying is that at the very heart of Vedanta is the idea that you are not to identify yourself with your thoughts alone. In fact, our thoughts and our mental concepts keep us limited. Our mind keeps spinning dreams, keeps spinning hopes, keeps spinning an enchanted view of life, and also very often an anxious view of life! But our reality is far greater than that. Knowing ourselves as *being beyond the mind,* we never become disillusioned, we never become disappointed. We don't become obsessed with what will happen tomorrow! Knowing that, a leader is able to act rightly and dynamically! A good leader is able to transcend anxious thoughts, and work from deep intuition rooted in the supreme consciousness within him or her, instead of acting from fluctuating feelings alone.

Mind does not have the wings to take us to ultimate freedom, to infinite spaces of our potential. The whole essence of Vedanta's meditative attitude is the process of stepping out of the mind, of moving beyond the cycle of thoughts. Every leader should have that vision: of being able to move outside the cycle of his or her own thoughts. That is the very crux of expansion at the mental level, and to expand at the mental level is to have vision. Only a visionary leader can expand towards a fuller vision of goals/aims/methodologies to achieve those goals and aims. Expansion is the secret: going beyond limited thought constructs. Especially in this age of rapid change and 'disruption', it is vital for a leader to understand and internalize this concept of Vedanta.

In other words, don't live in the ignorance that your thoughts are your ultimate reality! Thoughts can be limiting. They can condition you to standard ways of thinking, when what great leadership requires is always thinking out of the box, innovatively and dynamically. People who are true innovators, people who are true leaders/thought leaders, are able to go beyond the mental bondage of limited thoughts. They're able to go beyond the cage of limited thoughts and fly into the open sky of vision; into the open sky of being; into the greater dimensions of reality. And within that greater dimension of reality, they act with great freedom. That is what the essence of Vedanta is—pure witness-ship of yourself, seeing yourself as being comprised not only of mind but as being comprised of a greater universal energy. When you realize that, you find more and more insights happening to you.

A great leader must be an insightful leader. One who has what have been described as the 'eureka' or breakthrough moments of deep insight into problems, in order to solve them effectively. Now, usually, people are constantly repeating their own thoughts. We are consciously or unconsciously trapped in our own web of thoughts. The 'eureka' or breakthrough moments happen when we are able to find a higher consciousness than what our brain is able to suggest to us, and that is the true hallmark of a good leader. Intelligence is not our mental faculty alone, according to Vedanta. The intelligence of the leader needs to be identified with universal energy itself, on the intuitive plane. The truly great leader, according to Vedanta, acts as an instrument of this higher intelligence. Call it cosmic intelligence, call it universal intuitive intelligence, and so on. That intuitive intelligence is really what our *swabhav* or self-nature is. Our self-nature, as described in the Upanishads, as described in the Bhagavad-Gita, as described in the Yoga Vasishtha, as described in the Ashtavakra Gita, and in all other Vedantic texts, is that which is not bound by the mind. No! Our self-nature is that aspect of ourselves which encompasses truth, bliss, and consciousness. In other words, *sat-chit-ananda*. If you identify with the mind and thoughts alone you cannot move on to sat-chit-ananda; you cannot move on to the greater truth, the greater consciousness, and the greater bliss of life. And if a leader is not able to do that, how can he or she expect to take others towards a greater plane of functioning?

A leader's job is to inspire people, but if a leader is not inspired in their own self-vision, how can they inspire others? Adi Shankara says, 'Move, open your eyes to the greater mystery of existence—where the mind itself disappears; where the mind dissolves in the greatness of reality; where the drop realizes it's part of an infinity of the ocean of consciousness.' So know yourself to be part of the ocean of consciousness. Then you become blissful. Then you transcend your ordinary vision and your ordinary state of being, and you know your energies to be unlimited.

In other words, the crux of it all is to free your mind! Once you free your mind, you are able to move on to the next level of consciousness. And a truly visionary leader is one who is able to free their mind onto a state of higher consciousness. The greatest leaders, of course, move on to a state of super-consciousness, knowing themselves to be transcendent, unlimited, beyond the mind. Truly inspired leaders work from the super-conscious plane, inspired by higher purpose and intuition. That leads to game-changing moments.

The great Gautam Buddha used to say that the only difference between a Buddha and others, is that the Buddha knows he is a Buddha, and the others don't know that they are Buddhas! To do that—to know your higher spiritual nature or Buddha nature—you must go beyond the ordinary complexes and habits of the mind. This spiritual nature or Buddha nature means going beyond the ordinary complexes, the ordinary functioning of consciousness, and seeing that our human capacity for consciousness is capable of an infiniteness of perception, an infinite energy, an infinite sense of belonging to the vaster! These create a broad vista of leadership vision within the individual, and essentially, a good leader is one who can take people onto vaster realms of fulfilment.

The one great spiritual quality when it comes to leaders, is that he or she should be able to bring transformative and dynamic change for the better. To make such a transformative and dynamic change, it is very essential that the leader is able to go beyond his or her own prejudices and free the mind into acting with a greater sense of cooperation, a greater sense of empathy with others that itself leads to the betterment of all.

Adi Shankara says, 'The ignorant long for results and engage in action with the idea of "doership" and "enjoyership". The ignorant are deluded and think "I act", "I cause others to act", "I enjoy", "I cause others to enjoy", and so on!' Hence, Adi Shankara is saying that the whole 'I'-feeling limits us and keeps us ignorant! This is a very important point to understand when it comes to leadership. The 'I' complex of the truly great leader needs to be dissolved. A leader who is obsessed with the 'I' is only acting out of egoistic understanding. He or she is making themselves the entire centre of things, and that is the biggest delusion in life. Our biggest and most limiting factor is being caught up in this 'I' centre of being. A selfish leader acts from the 'I'; a good leader acts from the sense of 'we'. And 'we' implies the team. 'We' implies broader society. 'We' can also imply the cosmic family that we are all part of.

Eventually, none of us are the ultimate 'doers' in this magnificent universe. We must play our parts well, but must not be arrogant enough to think that it is 'I' who creates results. Humility of attitude makes for good leadership, because it makes us work with greater integrity, feeling that we have been entrusted a noble task by a greater cosmic power. According to Vedanta, we are just witnesses of this power unfolding and acting in the world. And our job is to do what we have to do, remembering that we are mere instruments and witnesses of this greater reality, which is moving the cosmos. That is the road towards optimum living. That is the key to higher fulfilment, not only at the individual level, but as an influencer for others also.

Hence, you can see that the sense of doership and 'I'-ship needs to be cut out if you are to act from a higher sensibility of leadership. Only through removing the 'I' is your anxiety reduced and you become centred and still in your being. The person who is constantly obsessed with the 'I' is never still, is never calm. A good leader needs to be calm and dynamic at the same time. So to attain calmness, it is very important to understand that this 'I'-centric feeling needs to be cut at the roots. Then anxious thoughts/fears and so on, do not affect one. One is never frustrated because one is able to think beyond the individual and think of the larger good. And a great leader is one who can think of the larger perspective. That is what differentiates true leaders from the rest of the people. This is something which the Buddha also emphasized. In fact, the Buddha echoed a lot of the old Vedanta concepts, especially when it came to weeding out this sense of 'I' at the centre of all things.

In a way, the whole 'I'-centred outlook is at the heart of the leadership crisis in the globe. Many leaders are so obsessed with the 'I' that they never really think about the 'we'. They're never really purposeful about taking society into greater heights of material and spiritual fulfilment. Now, to a very limited degree, the 'I' complex is important because it allows us to survive: we do that which is best for each of us to survive individually. But to be a truly great and profound leader, requires a certain broadness of vision.

We can look at the example of Nelson Mandela. He was always interested in expanding the vista of consciousness. That was his whole life's effort; and through that he could be a leader who was accepted by all strata of society in

South Africa. Eventually, he came to be respected even by those who were once antithetical to him, those who were once his supposed enemies. The people who had imprisoned him came to realize their foolishness, and it is primarily because Nelson Mandela exhibited some of those qualities which Vedanta talks about—this sense of expansiveness beyond the individual self, and into the broader cosmic self, which includes the collective.

Eventually, we are just a microcosm of the vast macrocosm that is existence. Let us not mistake ourselves to be the centre of all things—that gives us grief. It is like Arjun on the battlefield of Kurukshetra in the Mahabharat. He is so caught up in the 'I'—*his* anxieties/ frustrations, *his* fears, *his* concern for others, and so on— that he is not able to fight to his maximum ability. Once he is able to see the broader picture of things, that he is fighting a war for justice which will eventually set a good example for all concerned, is when he becomes free from his limited concepts! And then he acts out of great dynamism! He becomes a true leader on the battlefield. Yet he does all this with a calmness of being. Where does this calmness come from? It comes when he pulsates with the greater energy of knowing himself as being simply an instrument of the greater. And this is the entire basis of mysticism in Vedanta. This is the mysticism which Adi Shankaracharya wanted to teach people, because he knew that it would strengthen people at the root level. It makes people understand that they are much more than they think they are; that they can have a higher understanding, a broader understanding; that they can go beyond the ego; that they can go to a state which encompasses the wisdom of the broader. And so doing, not only do they become inwardly rich, but outwardly too, because in material action also they become far more dynamic and courageous. So these two aspects—inward richness and outer dynamism—are the two prongs of Vedanta. Each is complementary to the other. Hence, it is very important for us to self-realize this inner richness, in order to be outwardly dynamic, effective/great leaders in our own fields, and truly successful.

Team as a Fellowship

LESSON: Especially during tough situations, it becomes imperative to re-assert and strengthen the subtle energy field of our teams. Vedanta is eventually about harmonization of energies: this becomes key for empowering our group efforts.

Great leaders make teamwork into a feeling of fellowship, of belonging together for a common cause. This creates fortitude and strength in the team. The Vedantic concepts of *sadbhavana* and *sahacarya*, of fellowship and of belonging to a common human family, always echo this universal sentiment of fellowship.

The new paradigm of teamwork is of being a very democratic one. But it actually reflects the spirit of teamwork as exemplified in the code of the warrior of ancient India. On the battlefield, the force is to function as one singular entity, with fellowship. Each person's energy is to dissolve in the totality of the team effort. One's sense of individuality is to pool into a common pool of energy, so that each person becomes the support to others. It is very important to understand this concept of mutual support: each person does their best in their individual capacity, but is available to all the others as a support system. So it's like an organic entity, a forest where different trees exist, but all actually coexist within the same ecosystem. And through their own individual capacity, also enrich the common ground upon which they are all standing. Then only is an ecosystem a truly efficient ecosystem. And that is what a good team is supposed to be: an organic whole that is deeply rooted in an interdependency of friendship.

So bring this quality to the team. It's really what fulfils it at every level: result-wise, emotion-wise, intelligence-wise. This means that each one's doors have to be open to the others, so that there's a feeling of deep connection. Otherwise what happens is that people function fine as individual energies, but they're not able to pool in their energy efficiently enough. And teamwork is essentially about being able to pool energy together to make it a central source of shared energy.

So the concern is not just with the results, but with each other. It's about lifting each other in an attitude of devotion to the task, but also of mutual trust. That is what makes and differentiates an extraordinary team from an ordinary one. This quality of the heart—if you can call it that—is still the differentiator. It engenders a passion for excellence. It infuses a different vigour, fortitude, and strength within the team. Channels of communication open up, which perhaps we might not have expected normally. So it's a question of being able to flow into this common source of energy, being open to it. Hence, when you meet each other or communicate with each other within the team, it does not seem like much of an effort.

Most communication between people is non-verbal. It is at the level of body language and overall attitudes. So it is about conveying energy more than anything else. And that is what a good leader must seek to address, to create a fellowship within the team.

The team leader is responsible for the dynamic of energy, the interplay of energy, which is constantly a part of any group dynamic. The team leader should not look upon his role as a person who runs the entire team himself or herself. In fact, it is the team dynamic which should run the team. That is what efficiency in leadership means. Otherwise it leads to ego problems.

There are too many leaders who feel that they have to

shoulder the whole burden of giving the team a direction. But really a leader has to look upon herself or himself as a catalyst who can create the right conditions for this group dynamic to become positive. It is not about trying to run all the things within the group by oneself. Then there is a dictatorship. That is not the new paradigm of helpful coexistence. Working together to fulfil a common mission—that is the nature of true collaboration.

The future of mankind needs to be led by leaders who are positive collaborators. Essentially, a leader is a collaborator who catalyzes the group energy or team, giving spark to it. He should not try to impress his ideas upon the group as a dictator, and the group should not just really commit itself to one individual. Otherwise the exercise can become more about pleasing the leader instead of achieving the desired results.

So this is what we must learn: to raise up the energy of the entire fellowship, but not keep ourselves as separate egos within it. Instead, realize the team unit to be an extension of shared energies. It is like different rivers flowing into the same ocean. But the ocean is one, even though different sources have contributed to it! In other words, the spirit of the fellowship has to be one. Then only can it be a good team. Otherwise, there are too many guiding lights or guiding spirits to the team effort.

Everybody wants to be a leader, but the central 'spirit

of the team' is the important thing. And that itself can become the guiding light of the team. Sometimes we don't realize why one team performs better than others, even if the individual members of that particular team are not as good as the individuals of the other team are. Perhaps they are not perceived as being as efficient, as famous as the members of the other team. And this is what happens on the sports field—you find some teams sometimes consisting of superstars but when they come together, they are not able to function in tandem. The reason is simple: they are not able to pool their energy into the task as a singular whole. They function as individual guiding lights for the spirit of the team, but the spirit of the team itself goes missing. That is why they are often defeated by teams who are not comprised of very well-known individuals, but who have the ability to function with a common zest and zeal of spirit or purpose.

This same principle is what makes great armies and fighting units. Hence, you will find that very efficiently organized small groups of warriors can often be a great hindrance and formidable opponent to much larger armies. This is what happened between Rana Pratap and Akbar at the Battle of Haldighati. This is also what happened between Porus and Alexander. You can also see what happened between the Spartans and the Persians. And in the Mahabharat, you see that even though the Kaurav army was much bigger—and in fact had more individual heroes—it was the Pandavas who achieved victory. This is because of the central spirit of Dharma which guided them. So you should essentially see Dharma as the spirit of teamwork. This implies a spirit of fellowship, of real 'team spirit'.

Swan and Lotus:
The Alchemy of Symbols

LESSON: Vedanta's symbols are deep indicators of the qualities needed for excellence, success and leadership greatness: deep conviction, creating inner joy for outer affluence, and the ability to prosper amidst all crises or tough times.

"O Ram, even ignorant people can convert—by the power of their conviction—the poison into nectar!"
Yoga Vasishtha

The Swan (*Hansa*) and the Lotus (*Kamal*) are symbols used in Vedanta. These are simply representative of states of mind and spirit. Both symbolize the state of mental and spiritual purity:

the idea being that we human beings in our everyday lives can emulate the values these two symbols represent, in a manner which makes us more fulfilled, productive, and creative. Both symbols are meant to signify that one can be a positive contributor—and a source of great creative energy—in the middle of *any situation* that one is placed in. They signify that we can blossom to the fullest of our potential and ability even in the midst of a crisis, difficult situations, or tough times! In fact, that is just what good leaders need to do. Hence, these ideas of the swan and the lotus are powerful symbols for leaders—and for all those pursuing excellence—to emulate!

Both these symbols are not aggressive symbols. What they contain is something of the spiritual, of the beyond, something of the higher yet somehow humble. So the idea is that the mind can be in a very high state of functioning, can be capable of creativity, but at the same time capable of being of a certain grace and humbleness. So should a leader be. Like the swan which yearns to migrate to the clear waters of Mansarovar lake, yet while living in the ordinary world still manifests great power and virtue, so should a leader be: working to the best capacity in the world but always having a yearning for the greater. And like the lotus: humble, untouched by circumstances, yet working with maximum energy, inner grace, and power to achieve great results amidst all conditions.

All good things arise out of the pure space within us. Have the courage to work out of this purity of inner space, and then only do you become that which you were always meant to be. That is the spirit of the Swan and the Lotus. Greatness can manifest anywhere. You do not need the perfect conditions for it. You do not need any particular environment for it to happen. You can create this environment within yourself, and through creating it within yourself, positively affect all those that come within your range of action. So the symbols have a very subjective meaning: they are poetic, but they're also very practical as a lesson for work and life.

In Indian mythology the word for the world conqueror is *chakravartin*. But surprisingly, this title of chakravartin has been given not only to kings but also to mystics. So it implies leadership in the material sphere as well as in the psycho-spiritual sphere. Eventually, a 'world conqueror' means a person who is willing to lead in such a manner that sets a powerful and purposeful example to others. It is not to be taken literally. It is, in a sense, about conquering our negative parts and emphasizing the positive. That is said to be true Dharma, and implies that one does not have to be overly aggressive in one's style. In fact, the contrary may be true. One may exhibit only that which needs to be exhibited, but at the same time one should build up an inner fortitude, for that is the main thing which shapes the character of a great leader.

It is very interesting to note that in Eastern mythology, there exists a myth parallel to that in Western mythology—the story about the Philosopher's Stone or 'Paras Mani', which magically transforms the ordinary into the extraordinary or iron into gold. This is a very powerful symbolic story because it talks about an alchemical process of inner transformation. A transformation of attitude. So that we awaken to our own reality of being much greater than we ordinarily perceive ourselves to be. We are born spiritually noble, and we must emphasize that part of ours which is more than thoughts, material possessions, physical appearance, and character even. Do not define yourself in limitations, and you will automatically and spontaneously become unlimited in scope of action.

Symbols have hidden occult and oracular meanings. If we are only able to read into them, we would find that they are a template for many of the things that modern psychologists—such as Jung, Freud, as well as several neuroscientists—have been telling us. At a very subconscious and unconscious level we are part of the collective dream of the entire humanity. And that dream is of a spiritual evolution. And this evolution is one toward psychological, emotional, and spiritual clarity that enables us to fulfil our potential. Primarily, symbols and parables teach us how we can adapt and face up to crisis of all kinds. That is essentially what good leadership is to be: one's highest and most natural self in the middle of any crisis. Through that only can we help others.

Similarly, the avatars of Vishnu are taken in the Vedantic sense to be symbols of the heroic evolution of mankind. Taken at a very human level, we can relate to stories of the avatars and heroes who battle the odds and yet come out victorious. Much like the lotus does in the middle of all the muck surrounding it. Even the symbolism of 'heaven' and 'hell' is principally to tell us about the state of being we can create within our own lives. So again, the concept of the various heaven and hells as known in mythology is very symbolic and metaphorical. We can create our own heaven here and now within ourselves. By bringing a certain coolness and transcendent state of mind, by not being anxious about any situation which we might be confronted with, by not losing hope about any situations we may face but constantly keeping a positive face. That is what a leader must do: transmit hope to others. That is his or her fundamental duty, not to create a hell of uncertainty, hopelessness, chaos, and anxiety. A negative leader is one who creates mistrust, and keeps hope away from people, so that he can become powerful. Now, it's always our own choice: what kind of leaders we choose to be. But the beautiful part is that if we take on the attributes of spiritually-inspired positive leadership, our lives become richer in every manner.

CHAPTER-4

Realize Your Own
Inner Power

*LESSON: The Vedic and Upanishadic wisdom
of India finds highest expression through Vedanta's
teaching of how close our own soul already is to the
cosmic supersoul or divine entity. Knowing this fills one
with great faith, determination, strength, and courage. It
is the bedrock of the qualities that make great
leaders and truly successful people.*

"Enliven noble qualities and vitalize the
intellects of men. Rouse up heroes!
Enliven and put strength into the
masses of people!"
Rig Veda

Vedanta is very clear about one thing—that one is only to realize one's own cosmically gifted divine powers. We are already filled with great and intense powers within ourselves, and all of life is merely an opportunity to realize that. Therefore, it is not really possible to become part of the divine, since we already are that now. This is a very important insight with regard to the question of leadership and success, because most people have the idea that they can't do very much on their own. Without a realization of our own infinity we are very ordinary. The extraordinary happens, transformation happens within us when we realize that there is a space within us which is beyond time, beyond change, and beyond circumstance. We must have this very feeling in our heart—to become filled with the belief that we can be as great as the greatest person that has ever lived. This is not meant to be an egotistical thing, but is at the root of the confidence needed for good leadership. It is a big differentiator. And this confidence is meant to be born of internalization, of inner silence, of peacefulness.

Often, people have a very artificial or cultivated confidence. They try to impose self-importance from the outside. But it is very different to manifest this from the inside. All good things have to begin from within us, and then spread outwards. Growth happens from the interior to the exterior, from the roots to the branches.

Believe that you are a part of the eternal. Most people are being pulled in different directions by their various desires, thoughts, memories, and expectations. Very few people are at peace. Very few people have the ability within themselves to feel fulfilled even when alone, and that is the test of a good leader or person of excellence. Whether there are people to watch or not, there is such a confidence in being part of this infinite marvel called the universe.

It's the ability to look at the world and ourselves as part of a wonderful creation. Then only can new horizons open up to you. The Upanishads say, '*Aham Brahmasmi*'— 'I am the ultimate truth.' Even other religions echo the same thing: Jesus says, 'The kingdom of God is within you', the Sufi Mansour says, '*An al-Haq*.' So the essential thing is that you realize your own significance and truth, and begin to live with such vitality and gusto that the qualities of leadership spontaneously manifest more and more within you.

This exercise in realizing your divine power within is not to nourish your ego. It is simply exalting your own sense of being so that you can look to the higher. It is doing away with the complexes engendered by wrong beliefs. Negative leadership is that which seeks to reduce the other and exalt oneself. Positive leadership is that which seeks to uplift others as well as oneself. And you can only uplift others if your own eyes are uplifted to a higher place. To be uplifted in your vision, understand that you are part of this infinity of existence. You must join it and manifest its best qualities within yourselves. Also, one of the most important things is to forget the past and begin anew with the new vision of yourself as if you are born today. This feeling of renewal allows the energy to vibrate with great force. As a leader, to feel the power of your own individuality—or self-power—is the key.

The Vedantic vision is to go beyond your limitations, to be receptive to the highest truth within yourself. It implies understanding that life is a great gift which is given to us. You do have power enough to stand alone. You as an individual need not be dependent on anybody, but only on that which is within you. Ordinary people depend on others, but the real leader understands what individuality means in a spiritual sense. It simply means not wanting to depend emotionally. You have only yourself to fall back upon, and what existence has given you is enough. Nothing else is needed.

Life needs to be an evolution towards clarity. Through clarity we can connect with the greater picture—the larger, the cosmic, the universal consciousness—within us and become one with it. It is only because we forget this that we lose the passion to truly excel as human beings.

Excellence implies the ability to deeply look within the heart of your being, to find that real treasure which is within you. It cannot be found on the outside. It is there within. We are born with infinite capacity, but we always look for its false substitute in the outer world. The real search always begins within. That can be the greatest magic because it releases our founts of abundant energy within. The path to excellence is not on any outer road, but on the roads to the innermost self, where dwells the ultimate and real prayer. In Vedanta it is defined not as a prayer to any outward entity, but to that entity which exists within ourselves and has always existed within ourselves. Whatever our pattern of outward behaviour, is an effect of this self-realization. Those who are creative in leadership tap into this innermost source in a manner which is spiritual. They become receptive to the transformative power within themselves because that is the closest thing to perfection that we can know in reality.

CHAPTER - 5

The Clear Mind

LESSON: Vedanta stands for that clear-cut clarity which differentiates the greatest leaders from the mediocre ones. From this clarity springs forth wholeness and goodness in leadership thought and action.

The mind of the leader needs to be clear (*sahaj*) and unclouded (*nishkalank*). Now, this is easy to do when we are not in a difficulty, when circumstances are favourable. But when there is anguish, when there is challenge of any kind, then it becomes difficult to remain unclouded mentally and spiritually. In good times we can afford to be distracted even. It does not make much of a difference. But always remember that it is painful situations which give us depth and allow us to move toward real, unclouded clarity of mind.

In the old Vedanta philosophy, it is said that pain of any kind is a fire for purification. It is not meaningless; it is not purposeless. It has a certain mission to accomplish, because in difficult times we turn towards what is spiritually important for us. We begin taking the first steps. If we can remain unclouded in difficult moments, then we will not be distracted in our happy moments either. That is when the ability to remain truly unclouded will go deep within us.

A good leader always endeavours to make self-inquiry, and through self-inquiry comes the flowering of the inner-most. It is then that we transform potential into reality. The simple thing to remember is that those people who truly succeed first undergo tremendous transformation within themselves. This transformation is nothing but coming to a state where one is unclouded, one is undistracted, one is undisturbed and cool within. That quality strengthens, that quality is what creates real abundance-prosperity-peace in the outer realm. Without it, we are hampered in the performance of our leadership roles.

To be unclouded means you are in a state where you feel totally whole, and out of this wholeness comes the quality of true goodness in thought and action. It is the state where one does not bother so much about how others are reacting to you, but about flying to your utmost heights. It is a question of finding your own individuality or independence of spirit.

The tiger has been taken to be a symbol of individuality, courage, and independence of spirit since time immemorial in India, and particularly in Vedanta. The quality the tiger most represents is the ability to meet any challenge with completeness of energy! To not shy away from any challenge, but feel free in its functioning, not bothered about circumstances. This allows it to roam powerfully and almost king-like, and this king-like attitude is the height of both Vedanta and Raja Yoga (the king of yoga, the eight-fold path which is considered the pinnacle of all yogas). It signifies the ability to be noble—and to be our best—come what may! Used metaphorically, it's a symbol of being so unclouded in mind that one becomes deeply joyful, graceful, empowered inwardly, and dynamic!

Positive leadership in the Vedantic sense has also been likened to the relationship between the bee and the flower. The bee takes the nectar from the flower but does it with such skill that the flower is not harmed in any way. Such is the way of good and great leaders. They have the ability to create something out of whatever is available, but at the same time they are always positive in their contribution. They do not hurt the environment and people they exist with.

What are the characteristics of the unclouded mind? The first thing is that it has the ability to take the quantum leap, and to meet all challenges despite hesitations or uncertainties. The second thing is that it brings out something of the majestic which is hidden within. All spiritual philosophies of the world, not just Vedanta and Hindu mysticism, say that there resides a great kingdom within us, and all we have to do is to pursue this spiritual kingdom within. The very recognition of it makes us noble and dynamic in our lives. The third characteristic of the unclouded mind is that one is ready for anything. One is welcoming of things, because fear vanishes. Fear always vanishes in the clear light of understanding. That is a basic spiritual realization of the ancient Rishis. And when fear disappears, one becomes more courageous automatically, and people start being more loyal to one.

Loyalty is a very big factor when it comes to leadership. Some people seem to find it effortlessly. The secret lies in the unclouded mind. The leader who succeeds in having that attains the real treasure. Loyalty of spirit is the thing. It is the very foundation of great leadership, and also of great teamwork. Again, the best example given in the spiritual texts of Vedanta is that of honeybees. There is loyalty to one another amongst them as a team, but everyone knows their own role very clearly. They do not interfere with each other, but rather complement each others' energies.

Being unclouded means you get rid of that emotional and mental anxiety that is destroying your energy. Modern man is so filled with thoughts and responses to external things, that there is little space for being mentally and emotionally unclouded. We need to create a pure energy space within. This is a very subtle but important thing. Great leadership implies making a resolution that your energies will be unclouded within, in a purity of space within. Your energies will be flowing and dynamic from this moment onwards. You'll be throbbing with the positivity which comes with the clear, unclouded mind.

CHAPTER - 6

The Visionary Leader

LESSON: Looking at our life and leadership roles with such visionary freshness and insight that Vedanta stands for, has become increasingly important in our rapidly changing world.

Who is a visionary leader? A visionary leader is one who opens his or her eyes to the new constantly, and endeavours to open other people's eyes to the new as well. The difference between a visionary and others is that he or she is not attached to the past. From the point of view of Vedanta, this sense of detachment allows a person to look at things with fresh eyes. Life is a rapidly flowing movement, and in the world of business, of politics, this flow is extremely swift and dynamic. What was relevant yesterday is no longer relevant today, and will be even less relevant tomorrow.

But it is very important to understand the past in order to reconcile with the past, and through that to evolve a new vision. It is almost Freudian in nature: that we have to make peace with our past to move on with the new dynamically. There must be an emotional, psychological, and spiritual detachment. This quality has been constantly spoken about in Vedanta, in several sacred texts. Use your past experience, but do not let it constrain you psychologically or emotionally. Do not condition yourself, but transform yourself by learning from past experiences. Each past experience has been an opportunity for you to transform yourselves and to be something new.

It is like pure gold coming out through the process of fire: when the impurities have melted away. It is like a new sunrise. But for the sunrise of being to happen, you must have the quality of being able to go through an inward revolution. Inward revolution implies change in the structure of our consciousness. That is what spiritual evolution is. Only through this change in the structure of consciousness can come about true vision, something new in life. This is why spirituality is very important. It is vision-defining, not only at the level of our thoughts but about how we change our energies, about how we get prepared to go through circumstances. Our attitude should be one of transcending old ideas, so that the new can be born. There is great fulfilment, great beauty, and great joy in having a new vision and sharing it with others. Yet a lot of us are so subconsciously frustrated with things that have happened in the past, that we have lost patience with ourselves. And this very loss of patience is at the heart of not being able to be creative and visionary.

The key problem with man is that we want everything in a hurry, we want great things instantaneously. Great things do not happen unless one is in a state of inner patience. The seers or rishis of ancient India say that the more patience we have within us, the swifter do things happen! It is a misconception that an anxious state of being leads to fast results. A person who is centred and patient is always more efficient, and works in a more productive manner.

The other thing about vision is that the visionary must radiate a great sense of positivity all around. The visionary is not just concerned about his or her own goals but also about the presence he or she has with regard to energy. Some people do have vision but they do not give adequate energy to others, and then their vision comes to nothing. Vision demands sharing. Only then can the vision start becoming fulfilled. So sharing is the most important thing when it comes to being a visionary leader.

The path to greatness is the ability to keep sharing more and more. And this requires us to dissolve our ego (or *ahamkar* as it is called in Hindu philosophy and Vedanta). It requires magnanimity, generosity of heart and spirit.

The Vedantic view of the Absolute (Brahman) and even God is very interesting. It says that the Ultimate is inherent within each being in existence. So God is not an outward phenomenon, but is inside of everything. The inner nature of a tree, the inner nature of you and me: all things are part of the same spiritual aspect of reality. So sharing means connecting with the spiritual aspect. It is the progenitor of us all. With such a magnanimity of heart, a person is to share their vision in life. Then they automatically move towards stronger positions of leadership, because they have the ability to give off themselves more and more.

A real visionary is always interested in the aesthetic part of existence. In fact, they feel it is their duty to share their aesthetic sense in the best possible manner. A sense of sharing of aesthetic beauty and creativity marks the most positive of leaders. Steve Jobs, for example. The very basis of his company Apple was founded on these two attributes: beauty and creativity. And the mission was to share this aesthetic with as many people as possible. He remained not just a thinker but also a person very conscious of spreading aesthetic sensibility and something beautiful in the world through whatever means he could. Of course he chose technology, he chose gadgets, but the very basis of what he did has some spirituality inherent in it. Because his vision was founded upon the core concepts of Indian Vedanta and Japanese spirituality and mysticism.

Ultimately only that person can be truly happy who can create happiness for others. And there is no better way for a leader to do this than to share their greatest possible vision with whoever they can. The word for the spiritual visionaries of ancient India was Rishi. Now, Rishi literally means a visionary, a spiritual seer of truth. It means one who has a *drishti* or inner vision. This sense of vision has two aspects. The first thing is to be patient, collected, and silent within oneself, so that the vision dawns on one's being. And the second aspect is to share this vision freely! That, in fact, is what makes a good visionary in every field: be it politics, business, art, music, science, or any other human aspiration.

CHAPTER - 7

Balance and Watchfulness

LESSON: Maintaining balance and being watchful while dealing with problematic situations (or people) ensures effective leadership. It is at the core of India's Vedic and Vedantic scriptures. Balance generates true excellence and success.

The art of great leadership is the art of balance or *santulan*. The concept of mind-body-spirit *balance* is key in Vedanta, and runs as a common thread in most Hindu mystical philosophies. This concept of balance is a key part of the greatest Vedantic teachings, including those in the largest Vedanta text, the Yoga Vasishtha Maharamayan. This book contains detailed conversations on spirituality, life, and leadership between the sage Vasishtha and the young prince of Ayodhya, Sri Ram. Through this teaching of balance, Ram realizes the most profound truths for great leadership, and goes on to become the all-time leadership paragon of Indian civilization!

Essentially, in a leadership context, maintaining balance is all about seeing both the negative and the positive aspects of a situation as they are. It implies the ability to not get disturbed by either, and to maintain oneself in the middle ground mentally, essentially by being watchful. The way of watchfulness defines the art of balance. The way you observe things defines how delicately you can walk the 'tightrope' of life and leadership!

As a leader, you may have to constantly confront puzzling situations, which can potentially unbalance you. But a great commitment is required to keep the balance. See yourself as pure consciousness, which remains undisturbed by any material events on the one hand and any disturbance of thought or emotion on the other hand. That way, you become free to maintain an outlook that gives you more composure, more equilibrium, more steadiness.

Our work situations are often like a very disturbed and boisterous ocean, upon which we have to keep the boat afloat no matter what. Now, this does not require the leader to fight with any outer circumstance, but simply to find enough balance to stay afloat. It requires the leader to be in a state of inner harmony, that allows her or him to work with calm and in utmost peace. Because it is only in inner peace that we can remain in the centre, without the boat getting tossed to one side or the other. It is a question of centring yourself internally. If you are centred internally, you will also remain centred and steady on the path that you are walking. All your interactions and relationships at work, and in your personal space, will become more balanced.

Inner equilibrium leads to outer equilibrium. Emotional, mental, and spiritual stability are the keys to stability as a leader. And in the field of material leadership, the ability to maintain balance between work and relaxation gives rise to inner balance. Often, policymaking implementation and communication tend to escalate into rather unpleasant situations, simply because this element of balance within people goes missing. They precipitate situations because of a lack of inner equilibrium. They shoot out that nasty email, they say something which has repercussions that are unpleasant. It is essentially becoming a very unbalanced world on the whole, in every way. This is happening simply because the speed and ability to communicate has increased manifold in the past few years, and the inner psyche of man has not kept pace with the speed of material technology. So often, there is rather immature behaviour on display. Maturity in leadership is all about maintaining a steadiness, so that people respect you. Respect is a by-product of such steadiness. There needs to be harmony between what we think, what we do, and what we say. That is the only real way to succeed, and to be respected as a leader. Else down the line one would lose one's credibility. And so both material and spiritual balance are key. One of the biggest problems is that people function out of ego. They should not be doing so because ego is the quickest way to lose balance. Ego is the quickest way to fall. Dropping the ego is the only way to prevent the fall.

The modern workforce is rather complex—it is both structured and unstructured. A leader these days is expected to work well within the structure of the organization, but at the same time to work with such freedom that his or her innate ability of creativity is not compromised. One must lead, but without regimentation. Then only will good results come. At the same time, one has to create such an energy within one's team and groups, that they are also very harmonized, steady, balanced.

This balance—between structure and freedom—has to be struck, otherwise one can fall to either extreme (either being too regimented in one's attitude, or being too careless and unstructured in one's functioning). Without this balance, good results do not come. So, one has to be aware of this.

Also, if we were to use the classic example of the tightrope walker, we'd learn a great lesson about balance. The person who is walking the tightrope has to be both balanced and tranquil, calm—yet alert—within himself. If there is a disturbance in his balanced *inner state of being,* he's sure to fall. To maintain pure balanced consciousness, his breathing, his body, his feelings, his inner being, all have to be tranquil, calm, yet alert.

So remember, as a leader, to remind yourself of the key lesson of santulan or balance. Be relaxed. Be tranquil, yet alert. Also, *believe that you are totally capable of* walking the tightrope of life and leadership without feeling the heaviness of anxiety, or too many fluctuations of mood. Stay in the centre of yourself. Remember who you are, essentially. You are just a witnessing consciousness. With this attitude, no outer disturbance will be able to destroy your inner equilibrium. And a person who is in an inner equilibrium, is not destroyed by outer circumstances. In fact, he attains a great liberation of his potential. It is all about allowing the ego to disappear. It is all about working with joy, but also being attentive. At the same time, it is about being relaxed in your actions, but also being in an almost inward meditative state of consciousness. This allows you to be internally relaxed and restful, ensuring that you can move on with bliss and reach your goals without falling. It is Sri Ram's way of leadership, and is a great lesson to imbibe/emulate.

CHAPTER-8

The Seed of Infinite Consciousness

LESSON: Vedanta's greatest texts emphasize the ananta/ashesha or the infinite aspect of the human being's consciousness. When people cast off limitations and feel their infiniteness, they transcend and transform themselves! This principle is centric to Vedantic teaching, and key for leaders to absorb.

The entire goal of Vedanta and core Hindu spirituality is to make human beings feel unbounded and infinite. The real battle is always won in the consciousness of ourselves. It is about the inner depths of our consciousness speaking to us and working through us. Otherwise we remain very small in the scope of our work. The fundamental thing is to feel a sense of infiniteness. And through this come all the virtues of human beings, the primary one of which is determination and resolution.

Determination and resolution are the bedrock of great leadership, because leadership requires perseverance like nothing else. But it always begins as a seed in the consciousness of the leader. The preparation to do big things is to become noble in the vision of ourselves and of the world. And this nobility of vision is to feel that we are capable of the infinite. We represent it. Let this feeling spread out all over you. Let it echo through every cell of your being, and then you will become suffused with an energy which allows you to work with real diligence and tireless effort!

Being a spiritually inspired and evolved leader implies allowing the sun of consciousness to fully arise within you, so that you can also show light to others! Otherwise, if you yourself are in darkness, how will you lead others to a better place, or to better circumstances? The problem with several of today's leaders in various fields is that it often becomes a case of the blind leading the blind. So many problems in humanity are a result of this blindness and lack of positive leadership consciousness. Vedanta says that you have to create a good internal environment, a good internal milieu within yourself, and only then can you create positivity in the outside environment.

At the centre of this entire understanding of ourselves is attachment and identification with our failures and successes in life. We remain identified with what we have done and the results that these actions have given. So we have become result-oriented and not consciousness-oriented. The real spiritual secret is to become consciousness-oriented because that is also the primary seed of all results. As the seed is, so will the tree be! For us to manifest better actions as leaders—whether we are team leaders, society leaders, political leaders, business leaders of any sort—our concern must be that *we do not* become identified with our past successes or failures, but remember to keep moving on. And keep moving on in such a way that we can create more and more abundance for others, flowing along with us.

Vedanta believes in making each person his own or her own authority, without relying on outer teachings! It is about self-realization, and the pinnacle of self-realization is realizing the inner treasure which often remains hidden from our own view. So we have to transcend ourselves, our own conceptions. In transcending self-conceptions we go beyond ourselves, and help people go beyond their own limitations. It is a process of transformation.

In the old texts alchemy was called *rasayana*, the science of consciousness-transformation. In this science, the ideal of leadership is about being an alchemist who rises in his or her own potential, and allows others to rise through their's!

Vedanta keeps emphasizing that the ability to feel infinite is the most godly quality that we can have. Feeling limited and small is totally ungodly. Ironically, most religions say the opposite thing. Yet the Vedantic and Hindu view is not one of ego. In fact, it is the opposite. One is to feel so infinite that one just opens up to all that is. One is not to become limited by conditioning. That's what it truly means. One can still be humble, but it is like a flower opening its petals, and out of this opening comes a new state of being. It is the most important internal quality that is needed for a person to imbibe positive leadership virtues.

It is like climbing a mountain—we are not to become content without reaching the summit of ourselves. So consciousness is a summit which we need to scale, and at the pinnacle we will know the freedom of true release, of feeling infinite about ourselves. And through this very feeling is engendered and infused great confidence into those we interact with also, earning their respect. At a very fundamental psycho-spiritual level, this feeling of being infinite allows people to release their repressions, and to become what they're truly meant to be (in a state of freedom).

There are fundamentally two ways in which leaders

can choose to act: the first, the common way, is the one of aggression, and the other way is of having such confidence that one feels no need to be aggressive! One functions almost in a blissful state, but at the same time exudes a confidence that is almost divine. That is directly a result of feeling this sense of infiniteness within you. Psychologists say that the over-aggressive person is one who has a sense of less self-worth, whereas the unaggressive yet still effective person is one with a sense of higher self-worth. A person who can understand that he or she is fundamentally made of the same substance as the stars, of the cosmos, becomes unlimited by anything material that happens in the world, because in one's consciousness one transcends. A key Vedantic teaching from the Upanishads, '*Ayam Atma Brahma*!' It means that I am, at the level of soul, a part and parcel of the ultimate, highest, timeless, infinite being! So a leader is in a spiritual sense a seeker of the infinite, the timeless, the deathless, the source itself, of which all good things come. It is about following one's pure inner light, and through this very light comes about an intrinsic happiness. And spontaneously, positive results follow.

The greatest human achievements have always dawned from feelings of self-delight and self-infiniteness. With great composers, great scientists, inventors, or innovators, a large part of the inspiration came from this feeling of infinite potential. And through this, the confidence to achieve something truly creative arose! An innovative and creative leader should therefore work toward realizing such inspiration. Only then would she or he feel fully spiritually rejuvenated enough to take on any task.

CHAPTER-9

Peak Energy and
Non-Duality (Advaita)

LESSON: Advaita Vedanta is perhaps the greatest philosophy mankind has ever known: its implications for leaders and the subject of leadership energy are profound. Take away the tension surrounding much of our anxiety-oriented thought processes, and we attain great energy!

Most tension is created as a result of thinking about what will happen in the future! Why does the human being constantly miss opportunities for self-understanding, for growth, for insights, for evolving into his or her highest potential at work and life? It's simply because there's a concern, and almost an obsession with, what is going to happen! 'What if we fail?' This question is often the reason why most people do not evolve as good leaders. Because they are constantly trembling and calculating about whether they'll be able to fulfil themselves at a future date or not. And with this thought in mind, they are not able to achieve peak moments of energy (feeling depleted of energy).

A good leader is one who keeps energy levels very high. But the shortest way to lose energy and feel weak is to be too concerned about what is to come. Now, it is not a question of responsibility—*all of us must shoulder the responsibility of creating a better future.* But the simple fact is that the future is only born of the present. So in order to be the best that we can be at this moment, we must sow the seeds of courage. We are to do this simply by availing whatever energy there is in the here and now, fully.

If a real depthful examination of our mind processes is done in the technologically more advanced future, it may be found that the brain is fragmented or split between future, past, and present. Very rare are those people who can function with the purity of energy which is non-dual. What is the concept of non-duality? It is to make your energy as one, and this concept of non-duality is what the ancient Advaita Vedanta is all about. It's essentially about integrating your energies together, and of making the mind truly unified. This leads to a better understanding of reality. And it is the quality which leaders need to cultivate within themselves. It is the very basis of calmness, and decisive action is ultimately about calmness. The Yoga Vasishtha says, 'If one realizes the unity of things, one remains inwardly calm, cool, pure!'

While doing a task, it is not just the effort that we invest in the task that gives us results. More importantly, it is the harmony of energy that we bring to the task that ensures whether it'll be successful or not. Too often in the accomplishment of a task we are either working with a sense of inferiority (doubting future results), or working with a sense of superiority (being overconfident of what the results will be in the future). But the mature leader is one who does not go to either extreme, who does not go through any complex of either hopelessness or overconfidence. And that only comes when a greater awareness is concentrated on the work that is presently being done rather than on future happenings. This is in fact a great secret to success in human life.

Truly great people tend to have a total intoxication or trance-like state—almost a divine devotion—to the tasks they are accomplishing within the present moment. They remain absorbed in present-moment attentiveness instead of obsessing about past or future so much. You can examine the lives of all great people in the past. They took their particular tasks to be something which gave them great joy, and through this feeling of being completely and joyfully involved in the accomplishing of the present-moment task, their work automatically turned into something very valuable. The results simply followed into being extraordinary! (To draw an analogy with Abrahamic religions, it is almost like Jesus turning the water into wine: even the ordinary becoming extraordinary!)

Every human being carries infinite potential, but to actualize that potential what we really need is to crystallize our energy into a oneness, and that oneness can only come about if we are not self-conscious about whether we will achieve the desired results or not. So we are to remain in a natural state mentally. We are almost to surrender to the task at hand. We are to have a feeling of devotion to the task at hand. And through this devotion comes tremendous effort, which does not really feel like effort, but feels more like passionate involvement. Great results follow such an attitude towards work.

The same principle applies to leadership. Great leadership implies discontinuing the habit of associating yourself with anxieties about past or future. You are to bring yourself back to your roots of present-moment awareness. It is very important for a leader to be rooted, because only then can you focus your energies on leading within the present moment.

Do not trap yourself in the prison of the future. It is

an illusion. Remind yourself that all you have is the *now*. With this reminder, you are brought back to reality in a manner which enhances the value of the moment. It creates an urgency and energy in what you are doing. The problem with people is that they become so insecure that they cling to future results, and insecurity is the opposite of spirituality. It does not allow you to bloom to your utmost. So most people are very hesitant in their actions. They do not complete tasks properly simply because of this one factor—they are investing too much of the thought process in the future, and because of this they are always insecure.

Because the future is unknown and uncertain, the only certainty we have is the now, the present moment. And in that present moment, a great transformation of your being can come about. In present-moment awareness, if you are happily concentrated and focused, you do not feel any sense of rejection or failure. Because you become spontaneous, and your activity becomes spontaneous. An inner attitude of such spontaneity is very important in order to transform your future-oriented energies into present-oriented energies.

CHAPTER-10

Courage during Crisis

LESSON: Courage is the primary Vedantic step for excellence in life and leadership. In a world that has been shaken by such recent crises as pandemics, even more so!

The courage to make decisions in crisis situations, in a state of inward clarity, leads to great results in the end. The Vedantic parable of Ram and the story of Krishna remind us that *even the greatest personalities* made several decisions during crises that we can easily question. Yet eventually, victory was with them, and with those who listened to them.

Personally, these two avatars of the Supreme—Ram and Krishna—exemplified the highest virtues of existence even while living as human beings. They constantly set an example for us, that where there is the right intention infused with courage, there is nothing to fear. Victory is with those who are courageous and have values.

Crisis is defined in the old texts as a dark place, a dark situation, which can always be made luminous by the light of our own being. So basically, if a person is firmly rooted in values they can always grow out of crises. And the deeper the roots, the stronger does the tree become. So in fact crisis moments are an opportunity to dig our roots deeper, into a value system. Error in human beings primarily arises because we are not rooted enough. Hence, we do not really know how to grow out of the situations that seem full of trouble. And what is being rooted? Rootedness means you are completely immersed in the feeling that all things are born out of a greater power, and belong to a greater power. That is the divine attitude—to see oneness in diversity. If you are rooted in this way you are able to look at all circumstances as only different manifestations of the same energy, of which all things come and which permeates all things.

So we are to change our vision from looking at a crisis as something totally alien to us, something we cannot deal with, and instead look at it as something which is simply a part of this eternal and universal divine play that is taking place in existence. Then, we find ourselves moving away from fear and coming closer to our own sources of courage. Our mind becomes joyful, and we have the capacity to be joyful in the midst of any circumstance. Because we can look at things with the eye of awareness, with the eye of bliss, and are able to deal with reality as it is. So it simply depends on our level of awareness.

Do not become identified with the circumstances. During any moment of extreme joy, success, or failure, be even and tranquil in temperament. The problem with most people is that they start identifying with the circumstances, and in that very identification with circumstances they lose their inner rootedness to reality. So in the next moment, when something unfavourable may happen to them, they keep identifying with the problem, and identifying with it they lose their objective judgment to deal with it and thereby to transcend it.

Spirituality basically implies having a certain simplicity, clarity, and state of non-identification with whatever circumstances come your way. This is the one thing that leads to courage. This is the one thing that leads to wisdom and purity of insight. Success is never ultimately far from failure, and failure never far from crisis. It is our ability to look at it with clarity, that has real importance.

Be uncontaminated by circumstances, and they will cease to have power over you. Being uncontaminated means that in the deepest core of your being nothing should be able to hurt you. And this ability only arises if you have a feeling of detached freedom from whatever is going on in the outer world. Yes, be completely dynamic in the outer world of action, of materialism. But within yourself have the ability to see this: that it is the way the mind chooses to deal with things that helps determine outcomes.

If you truly want to be happy, nothing can stop you from being happy! Joy and sorrow are a part of creation, part of being. There is no need to be miserable when faced with crisis. This ability to see that there is always a choice, is when you begin transcending and start moving towards success, instead of simply being manipulated by outer circumstances and forces.

There are very few people who are not manipulated by things on the outside, who believe in themselves well enough to remain rational, to remain full of energy and bliss. Now, it is said that the only true prayer is that which arises out of a heart full of gratitude. So begin by being grateful for whatever it is you have. Try not to have a complaining attitude towards things. Through acceptance comes the ability to deal with things, while through rejection we carry on in the cycle of identification. Serenity, silence, and success always go hand in hand. He who knows this knows the art of moving out of the grip of circumstances, and starts referring instead to his own inner being in an objective manner.

A leader must have this objective ability to understand that no matter whether it is bright or dark, whether there are favourable or unfavourable circumstances, he always has the ability to shine his own inner source of light onto the circumstances. And so doing, to create a luminosity on the path that he's walking on and having others walk on. In other words, the leader is to become more involved with his intrinsic life-energy than to get affected by what material existence brings his way. Man has a tendency to brood and over-ponder about circumstances, and that is his biggest weakness. He often loses the ability to flow dynamically, with all the strength and courage of his being, because of this obsession with material circumstances. This needs to be overcome!

Vedanta is a going back to one's inner resources. Vedanta says that all material circumstance can be overcome and transcended through the spiritual perspective. Real strength is of the inner, and not so much of the outer. This is an essential principle to understand when it comes to leadership and success.

CHAPTER-11

The 'Guru' Is Within

LESSON: The Upanishads, from which the mystical philosophy of Vedanta comes, teach self-reliance in the realm of spirituality. The inner light of being is the guide! Great leaders have the ability of being self-illuminated.

It is very interesting to note that in ancient India there was one person in the court who even the king—while being the supreme leader—deferred to and listen to. That person of course was the Raj Guru, the royal sage. It was the Guru's responsibility to see that the king not only successfully led the people, but paid attention to the state of his own being. Because only through inner mastery can outer mastery happen.

So the Guru is basically a catalyst for both inner and outer dynamism. But the interesting part is that Indian mythology and spirituality, particularly Vedanta, asserts that ultimately the guru resides within oneself! And this guru is nothing but the voice of your consciousness. In other words, the guru is within you. This is a constant teaching of the Upanishads and Vedantic texts such as the Adhyatma Ramayana, the Ashtavakra Gita, and Yoga Vasishtha. Therefore, let your inner guru guide you to leadership wisdom and success!

It is said that the highest spiritual beings on earth—be they the rishis of India, Buddha, Jesus of Nazareth—all of these are depicted with halos around the heads. It is almost like that inner consciousness within them is shining so brightly outwardly, that they become luminous in the eyes of others. But to a lesser degree, luminous charisma is present in the personalities of all great people. They radiate some sort of charisma: in Abraham Lincoln for example, in Nelson Mandela, in Steve Jobs. This is the part of *inner luminosity* brought out by the inner spiritual sense of life they believed in. Jobs and Mandela for example looked to *an inner spiritual wisdom or inner guide*—an inner guru—to dictate their actions in the outer world. So doing, *we can also* become more spontaneous, more charismatic, and in fact more effortless.

The guru is symbolic of our own self-mirror. We have

to see our spiritual reflection within ourselves, and see ourselves as we really are. And thereby go on improving, go on wiping the mirror, so that our application of action is true and authentic, so that we retain our authenticity. That is the essential spiritual quest. It is also the greatest lesson for leadership: to retain your original face.

In fact, even the relationship between the king and the Raj Guru was born so that the king should be able to look at the Guru and find *his own truth* reflected, and not just listen blindly to the Guru. So essentially, the whole relationship between a guru and a leader is metaphorical. Eventually, 'guru' is simply a word or a device to remind us that we need to listen to the voice of the Atman or soul. We need to listen to that guide within, who's always residing in us. Make the ego subservient to the inner guide, and it'll lead you to real mastery in leadership. That is the essential lesson. It is about one's own conscience. It is essentially the spirit— the spiritual 'heart' of man—which should be the master over one's being. Because then one will be going in the right direction.

Once you come to this root, your whole leadership style would take on a different level of passion, a different level of warmth. Some passage will open which allows you to function with your heart to a greater degree. And when you can do that, everything becomes easier. Everything becomes possible and doable. The highest human virtues of courage, of hope, all live within the heart of human consciousness. Simply respond to it in the best manner possible. That is what it means to listen to your inner guide or guru. Essentially, it means that there's a divine presence within us, and that is the channel through which the energy of the greater flows.

Remain a student of yourself, a disciple of your inner wisdom. That is the way to constantly be a learner. Do not think you have mastered everything; there's a part of you which is hidden, which is higher and deeper than you are in your normal consciousness. Simply listen to it, and then your action becomes more integrated, wholesome, and positive. The problem with most of us is that we hardly listen to the inner guide with a great deal of conviction. People are too busy looking in the spiritual marketplace for gurus, but real transformation happens when the guru within is felt by yourself. You don't need an outside guru—because you yourself are unique, you are independent. Respect yourself, and out of that you'll automatically find respect in the outer world. Have faith in yourself, rely on yourself, have belief in yourself.

This is essentially the final word of spirituality: to be a guru of yourself. And yes, each of us has the capacity to be like that. Our inner guide is the golden compass, always pointing in the right direction. That is required for our own self-evolution, and for the evolution of people we work with, both materially and spiritually.

But the question is, how do we make contact with this inner guide? Well, it is actually very natural and simple. It's a question of not being too obsessed with outer abilities and outer mental functions. Work skills and technical skills are one thing as a leader, as is the ability to convince people. All this is part of leadership intelligence, yet there is something spiritual that is the strongest part of you as an individual. To find true fulfilment, you do not have to rely solely on your own mental cleverness or skills, but pay attention also to the spirit of spontaneous ability within yourself, which is your spiritual strength.

By being aware that you have a spiritual strength within you, you not only become more dynamic, but also full of a bright inner light and illuminating charisma which touches every aspect of your work. And which also reaches others. This force manifests as *prana*, *tejas*, and *ojas* in Vedantic mystic language, and *chi* in Chinese Taoist traditions. It is the manifestation of essential spiritual energy within us, which acts as our own guide. Follow that energy, and you will never go wrong. So anyway, it's about bridging your outer activity with your inner guide. So that the inner guide becomes the pathfinder, the light on the journey, and then you can walk with confidence for whatever you seek to do.

In Indian philosophy, and particularly in Vedantic philosophy, our innate wisdom—the great inner guru or guide—is to be invoked through intuitive self-reflection and internalization. This allows us to navigate the ocean of the material world with greater wisdom. The search for our deeper inner guru is essentially the search of all Vedanta, and indeed of all spirituality. The meaningful part for leaders is this: upon dynamizing your innate wisdom or core of being through self-reflection and internalization, your mental faculties and outer abilities as a leader also shine far brighter.

Transformational Leadership through Deep Listening

LESSON: The timeless lesson of paying deep and close attention is Vedanta's tool for cultivating insight and higher intelligence. The act of attentive listening is key to transformative and highly effective leadership.

In Vedanta, prayer is said to be not the act of 'speaking' to the *parama purusha*/Brahman (highest reality) but the act of concentrated 'listening' *(shravana)*. Through the act of concentrated, deep, and intense 'listening' to the cosmic message of nature/god do we attain true dynamism. Else, we are too engrossed listening to our own repetitive thoughts! Great innovators and leaders heed the 'greater voice', and thereby become visionaries. This is a cornerstone of good leadership: being in a state where we are open to the universal intelligence that is all around us and in us, and within which we exist. That is the way one's intuition and intelligence become evolved and visionary. That is also the way one can feel truly still within, peaceful, calm, meditative, energetic, and dynamic. That is also the way one's 'heart' becomes seeped in a deeper way into existence. So for dynamic leadership, that which is wholehearted and not half-hearted, it is imperative that we become concentrated listeners to *the inner voice of the beyond* that is always speaking in us and through us. Now, this same truth applied to the sages of ancient India, who are said to have listened to the entirety of the Vedic knowledge, intuiting and conveying it through their act of meditative listening to that which the Greater is conveying.

Basically, the art of deep listening implies paying attention to the higher consciousness hidden within ourselves, and being accepting of it. Out of such acceptance comes an inner relaxation and real understanding of reality. After all, what is intelligence? True intelligence means being free from any kind of conditioning, and responding to things as we encounter them. And that is also the hallmark of good leadership! It is all about being able to absorb more fully from one's environment, like a sponge. Through this inner absorption comes transformation and insight into how things really work. And this is the real art of listening: coming into a rhythmic understanding of all that is around us. That is the responsibility a good leader has to be alert to. Through this alertness, the leader is to create such insight that she or he can bring about order where there was disorder. In fact, the primary duty or Dharma of a leader is to create order where there is chaos.

So create a slight discipline about the act of listening. Be aware of its power. It will bring out a greater ability to read into things, and to respond in a manner which leads to greater success. Most good leaders have one very good quality in common: they can be extremely calm and cool in adverse situations. They seem very collected within themselves during crises. This ensures an unshakeable power within. This leads to what has been called 'right mindfulness', a state of being where total energy awakens within you, and you feel a sense of wholeness.

The best part of Hindu philosophy and Vedanta is that it has nothing to do with very particular beliefs or set of beliefs. Rather, it emphasizes the states of being. It talks about how you can move closer to your own ultimate potentiality, and also closer to the larger truth of existence. It does not teach anything novel, but tries to instil those timeless principles that can give us the taste of spiritual freedom, as well as take us to an unfolding of our own life skills. That is why it has been so universally resonant with people around the world.

In Vedanta it is said that what we have to do is find our original self which is hidden underneath several layers of conditioning. What listening attentively does, is to allow us to feel those layers, and to peel those layers. Ultimately coming to the core of ourselves. And coming to this very core of ourselves, we not only relate to ourselves better, but also relate to others in the material world in a much more mature and meaningful manner. Interestingly, Jesus also tells his disciples such a thing: that they 'hear but do not listen'. Vedanta philosophy also says that while we may be listening in a gross manner, the subtle art of deeper listening is to come to an inner silence and to act from that inner silence. Because acting from that pure space of inner silence allows the very spirit of ourselves—the very core of ourselves—to find splendid expression.

How many people work from their hearts? The main difference between geniuses and others is the genius' ability to go so deeply with their hearts into their pursuit, that spontaneously some new insights are born! And listening is the most accessible way of going deeply into a thing. It does not require much effort. It just requires a will to relate to others and to the world, in a manner which is much more meaningful. In fact, at some level all meditation is nothing but 'listening' to the silence within ourselves. Ultimately, listening to the silence within has the ability to rejuvenate and recreate us.

Vedanta says that we live within many circles of life. At the outermost circle is the material outer world. Within that circle is another circle, which is the circle of our own physical being. Within that also is the circle of our thoughts or ideas. Then is the circle of our feelings. And even subtler than feelings is the circle of the pure 'witness' within us. And that pure witness is the purest of things. So it's our job at our innermost core to listen to these different circles, all these different layers of our existence. If we listen close enough to people and events in the material world, we come closer to understanding our own thought process. In becoming closer to our thought processes we begin understanding our own feelings better, ultimately being able to access our core innermost intelligence of being a pure witness.

Hence, this act of concentrated listening and deep attention is very important for any leader. Spirituality is a growth process, and in order to grow, we need to put our entire heart and mind into something. We need great intensity. In fact, intensity is one of the hallmarks of good leadership. Without intensity, one remains unsure. But what is intensity? Intensity means wholeness and totality of being. And wholeness or totality are born from the act and art of listening totally! It is born from bringing higher consciousness to our listening, and making that a sustained effort. Then only is the bliss of relating to others truly meaningful. Somebody may say, 'What is the need for this sort of meditative listening; you just do what you like . . . Follow what your mind tells you as an individual.' But the fact is that we are interconnected at spiritual levels, not just mental levels. Hence, the truth of the matter is that for true inner silence and wisdom to be born, deep listening is important; for more profound understanding to be born, deep listening is important. Make it a habit. Real prayer is listening, real dynamic action begins with deep listening. This transforms all action into spontaneous, effortless action.

It is said in the oldest Vedantic texts that when you are really still and silent is when the voice of parama purusha or god speaks to you. You begin hearing and living in a totally different kind of way: your work is then not done out of a sense of just duty, but out of a sense of real spiritual joy. You thereby begin communicating better with the outside world, and within yourself. And that is key for effective leadership, excellence and true success!

CHAPTER-13

Your Light Within:
The Warrior's Way

LESSON: Vedanta is mysticism for both the sage and the warrior! That is what makes it unique. Its lessons of soulful self-awareness and blissful self-truth have the deepest implications for leaders.

Vedanta is the mystical science of paying attention to the indwelling spirit (atma) that is within us, and through that, doing good in the world. A key concept of Vedanta is that life is actually meaningless without paying attention to—and knowing—the entity of ultimate truth which resides within ourselves. We remain shallow if we do not come to that place within us which is of the nature of eternal light. Most people live their lives on the circumference of their beings, but quality in life and quality in action implies experiencing one's own light, one's own sense of eternity. That is when true purpose and meaning dawn on us. Therefore, to be a truly great leader, the goal is not to stop at being just wealthy or powerful, but to have the capacity to create bliss through whatever skills one has.

So the whole goal should be defined in terms of bliss, because bliss *(ananda)* is essentially our innermost nature. And bliss is also the result that should ideally come out of one's activities in the world. This is the true way of the warrior. Yes, one has to fight to win any battle in life, but the true victory is achieved only if one can conquer oneself. Because only then does one's true potential flow out into the world. Outer victory is meaningless without inner victory. Victory of the inner has to be a hallmark for truly great leadership to take place. Otherwise leadership can easily become an act of ego. It can become an act where one is trying to conquer things within the material world and control people, but with the sword of cleverness instead of the sharper sword of wisdom.

The great way to achieve victory is through the sword of truth and the sword of self-realization. It's about the well-being of our indwelling spirit. And what is the means to achieve the well-being of our indwelling spirit? The first thing is to do our work with such cheerfulness of heart that we come into tune with the rhythm of the world; that allows an explosion of our self-potential. Vedanta says that the whole cosmos is in a state of eternal joy; it is—in a symbolic way—in a state of dance and song. Through the sense of our own cheerfulness, we come into a true unity with that cosmic dance.

Hence, enter into the next level of consciousness, for through that next level of consciousness comes contentment at the layers of the material, the psychological, the emotional, the mental, and the spiritual being. So it basically means dissolving yourself, and finding that you are one with the nature of your indwelling spirit. Leadership that arises out of such consciousness brings you closer to your own potential greatness. The small impediments fall off from you; you start having a greater outpouring of energy.

Greater energy is to well up within you in order to be an effective leader. It is said in the ancient texts that both the ultimate spiritual truth and ultimate spiritual energy await you in your own heart. Yet we keep looking for these on the outside. Which is why we keep going against our own indwelling spirit. Our search becomes very external, whereas all that is needed is genuineness within ourselves. And that is the best feeling in the world: to be genuine, sincere, and honest enough to create fulfilment not only for yourself as a leader, but for everybody and everything that comes within your domain.

CHAPTER-14

Adi Shankara: Clear and Present Attention to Cosmic Oneness

LESSON: Vedanta is eventually about the meditative attitude, the intuitive oneness with all things. Through that comes joy, energy, intelligence, wisdom, strength, and enhancement of our life-force and leadership ability.

Adi Shankaracharya, the great Vedantin, always emphasized *oneness of being* with others. The concept of spiritual oneness *(ekbhava)* is based on the understanding that each one of us is a part of the cycle of the cosmos. We are not separate from the universe. We are an essential part of it. This implies that we are one with all the beings within the cosmos. Now, the basic problem on earth is that people consider themselves separate and divided from most other people. Hence, there is a constant clash, a constant conflict mentally. And religions as well as politics have sought to take advantage of this sense of separateness. Only then can they exploit people's sense of insecurity. But all separateness is illusory, says Vedanta. Adi Shankara constantly tried to make people understand that everything is one. When you understand this basic truth, your whole worldview changes. You stop looking at others as enemies. So your relationships start improving. This one basic understanding—this attention to oneness—can create a world where people are not just competing with each other, but co-operating with each other. This sense of co-operation, brought about by an inner inspiration of oneness, can create a great transformation in the human mind. It brings us closer to our own inner centre, but also connects us spiritually in a more heart-to-heart connect with the universe itself. Thereby, we begin to feel not only a greater sense of joy and an enhanced quality of living within ourselves, but also an ease of working with others. This ease of working with others is what the most successful people/leaders are able to discover.

Successful leaders and successful people in general know the art of co-operation. They know how to make others align with their objectives. It all begins by having the skill to connect at a deeper level. That is what 'people skills' are. That is what social skills essentially are. But this is spiritually at the heart of human behaviour. The idea is not to keep creating divisions in your consciousness, but to create integration within it. Through this integration comes about a great clarity and a great sense of involvement in the universe, as a creative part of it.

Ultimately it is our attitudes which determine the way we function in the outer sphere of being. That is why our sense of consciousness is so important. It was at the sensibility of consciousness that Shankara constantly tried to transform people. It was not about preaching a particular religion, it was not about preaching a particular way of life, but simply a revolution of consciousness which he aimed at. And one of the most fundamental things is this aspect of oneness, of co-operation.

A feeling of oneness, through the meditative or intuitively contemplative mental stance, is our bridge to the universe. It makes us drop fear because we know that all are a part of the same cosmic cycle. There is nobody who is spiritually against us, even if that may seem so. With this attitude, we are more at ease with others. And then our fear can vanish from within us. With the disappearance of fear, we can experience true stillness. On the other hand, with fear comes suspicion, inhibitions, and jealousy. And that makes human beings very restricted. The maximum causes for problems in the world begin with some sense of fear: people feel fear for another religion, another race, another lifestyle, and so on. Hence, there is constant conflict at our workplaces too. There are all sorts of fears and complexes at work. But it is only when this basic fear is removed—through the action of recognizing intrinsic oneness—that the human mind becomes filled with a renewed and fresh energy. That is when we feel our greatest powers.

It is very interesting that the word *siddhi* or super conscious power has been described in the old texts as a natural consequence of feeling, the sense of oneness with all things. Because then what happens is, you become an organic part of the entire cosmos at a deep psycho-spiritual level, and are able to harness and tap into its greater powers. It is really a metaphorical way of saying that to be nourished by the universe, we must nourish ourselves with the thought impulse of its intrinsic and essential oneness. Then we begin to experience—at a deep level of emotions, feelings, and spiritual impulses— that we are here for a purpose; that we are not helpless; that we can create and move together towards achieving important things, creating things of self-value and value to the world. With this sense of self-value comes about a great inspiration and energy to be a productive part of the material world.

So all things begin with an understanding that you are not alone, that everything is obtainable to you but only if you can see it and feel it deeply. By not feeling alone, suddenly you are filled with courage. A great sense of bravery crystallizes in you, and you are able to clearly move towards achieving your innate potential and your goals. It is simply a question of your quality of perception: of being able to see things in the right perspective. If a person sees himself as totally separate, it would look like people in the world are against him. And if a person can look at the whole universe as being part of his or her own family, one would automatically become friendly with others, more co-operative. Through this very co-operation comes absolute growth not only of oneself, but of whoever comes within one's material or psycho-spiritual sphere. And thereby, spontaneously, one attains leadership prowess because people respect such qualities and are attracted to them.

CHAPTER-15

All Great Action Is Born of the Meditative, Intuitive State

LESSON: Like the previous chapter has hinted, the root of all greatness is always the meditatively intuitive state. To be a more effective and truly great leader, cultivate this state of being within yourself.

In the spiritual philosophy of Vedanta, all great action is said to be born out of the meditative, intuitive state. Basically what it implies is that it is not the method of meditation itself, nor any technique of meditation, but essentially a discovery of one's own being which determines our outer action. Throughout his life, the great modern teacher of Vedanta, Swami Vivekananda, used to insist that his action in the material world is only a small manifestation of that which Master Ramakrishna impelled him to do in the meditative, intuitive state.

So, first is the meditative impulse, and then comes creative *(sarjanatmak)* action. Otherwise all action becomes non-original. Truly individual and original action is simply a flow of the soul's impulses—that which you perceive in your moments of deep inner silence. Out of that comes a deeper functioning of our material energies. So the idea is to be fully awake to your own inner silence. And when you become fully awake to your own inner silence, the core of you starts getting activated. It then commands the instruments of your body-mind complex to function in a manner which is not skin-deep, but which allows your best qualities to flow through.

From this point of view, it is not a question of your outward mental desires which should determine action. But in fact, it is desireless action which takes you to the ultimate peak of consciousness. And this is what even Krishna teaches in the Bhagavad Gita. Truly desireless action is meditative action. From the point of view of success and leadership, it implies that you activate your inner intelligence to a degree where your responses to situations are a reflection of what you really are, instead of being mechanical responses. So what this implies is that you are able to bring the completeness of your energies to that which you do. And where there is completeness of energies in action, you spontaneously move towards a fulfilment and success of intention.

The human being has such immense powers within himself, that if you are repressing them by only functioning out of external thought impulses, you are doing yourself a great disservice. The most positive force within you is the interior force or the spiritual force. There were several times in Vivekananda's life when he used to downplay the level of impact he had upon the world. In fact, he used to often say that he's much of a failure! Simply because he felt he was not able to directly transmit the lessons of consciousness and meditation more directly onto people. He felt he was sometimes not able to transform people from the inner as much as he would like. And that inner transformation, he said, was his most essential work. Yet if we examine his life in totality, we can easily see that it is a success in every way: at the level of name and fame that he gathered. And of course money was never an objective for him. Yet there were times when he needed money, especially for setting up the mission. And it flowed in from several directions, almost spontaneously. This was a material manifestation of his inner quality of meditativeness, and not so much of his wanting to dominate the material sphere.

Eventually, it is not about dominance of our ecosystem which should be the goal of the human being. That only creates more and more destructiveness in the ecosystem. In fact, it is at the root of so many human problems: be they environmental, political, religious, and so on. The act of meditation is really the act of inner evolution. And evolution is the key to developing as a successful human being.

Hence, if you want to participate in the material world to the maximum of your ability, tap into your meditative spaces. For there lies the master of your own destiny. Vedanta emphasizes that we are each masters of our own will and fate, but it's simply a question of *wanting* inner transformation! If only *we deeply want* a true alchemy to happen within ourselves, then does the alchemy of our mind-body-spirit complex begin to happen within the outer world. All that we touch in fact can turn to 'gold': through our relationships, through our networks of people. Because there is an essential power of spontaneous growth which comes out of the meditative space. It creates a luminosity of being, and people feel attracted to this radiance of being. You become charismatic; you become magnetic. And this ability to be charismatic and magnetic is an essential part of great leadership and excellence!

CHAPTER-16

Individual Greatness and Purpose

LESSON: You carry a small part of the very source from which all energy and all action comes. Yes, you do reflect the Absolute or the Supreme form in miniature within you. Hence, never doubt yourself when faced with life challenges! This is key for leaders at all levels to understand.

The beauty about Vedanta and Hindu mysticism is that there is no one *particular individual* conveyor of the Divine or *Brahman's* message, nor even a *particular group of teachers* of God's message. This is in fact one of Hinduism's most distinctive features: that each being is adept to bear the supreme divine message, and of living it! You are capable of higher purpose—of bearing your own personal message of the Supreme and of carrying out your own special work in this world, in your own way, through your own individuality *(vishistita)*! Realization of this is a great secret for making your life more purposeful and powerful, giving you real inner confidence as an achiever and leader.

Vedanta and Hindu mysticism emphasizes individual greatness. Through the very realization within the individual that she or he has some special work to give and purpose to be fulfilled, arises a great flow of consciousness and energy! And through this, a great force and will of being good leaders in our respective spheres of work, is born within us.

It is important at every stage of life to remember that no matter what our level of achievement, we are not to forget that we are each a unique light within the world! We are to shine that light not only for our own potential to be realized, but in some manner to bring something unique into the world. This realization is to be part of one's consciousness, because it is very empowering. This teaching must in fact become a part not only of education, but of continuing education for people, to be reminded that their lives have a certain unique purpose. Because then the qualities of leadership truly begin manifesting more and more, and there is a deep fulfilment of being—a harmony and rhythm that one experiences in one's life and work.

In the Hindu view, each *Atman* or soul is merely a reflection of the *Paramatman* or the divine. But this simple reflection is indeed very important, because it manifests the qualities of the greater—and through the action of these qualities one can bring about great transformation, great value within the world. It brings a deep capacity to see life in a greater and broader manner. One begins enjoying one's energies and appreciating them more. One attains the state of gratitude, and we must understand that gratitude is a very fundamental part of potential realization. In fact, modern neuroscience tells us that serotonin is secreted in the brain when we feel a sense of gratitude, leading to a great surge of happiness within. Through gratitude comes purpose-centred feeling. We can experience that as individuals—without it we would always feel deficient and lacking, and with such feeling of self-deficiency, truly positive leadership does not happen. Rather, it becomes negative. To be a leader is to be related to others. If we are relating to others when we are not in a state of fulfilment ourselves, how can we expect to convey something truly positive? And how can we lift the other person's actions, in order to fulfil goals. It is only when we feel, experience, and listen with a great sense of purpose, that we begin to assimilate not only a better understanding of what we ourselves are, but also become more creative in our ability within the material world.

The problem with a lot of leaders is that they often experience a lack of energy, a certain tiredness due to the constant clashes and conflicts that are happening in their workplace. Now, how do we transcend this constant feeling of tiredness, this fatigue which comes about through conflict, through friction? We have to experience the basic spiritual thing—feeling humble enough to understand that we are part of a greater design, yet at the same time acknowledge that we ourselves have a very important message to convey. This reconciliation of humility and self-realization creates a light within one's consciousness, and this light not only shines within and gives us joy but also shines bright in whatever worldly activity we undertake. So in a leadership role, at a very practical level, it is also very important. It determines the outcomes of that which we do. Then we are not trying to impose anything upon ourselves nor upon others, but simply functioning as if we are conveying a greater message, and conveying it happily. We begin doing so in an objective manner, in a manner that one's inner being is not tired. Because the inner being is now awakened to a greater consciousness of one's potential. This very realization creates energy, it creates a coolness, a calm kind of passion within us. And through this calm spiritual passion, energy is created.

The human being is in every way trying to achieve

either position, power, respectability, money, or happiness, but essentially the pursuit itself does not bring joy. What really brings joy is one's state of being within, and that is why spirituality is important, especially the spirituality of the ancient Vedanta of Hinduism. It says that you are not to worry about action itself. Action is born spontaneously, depending on how you look at the world and at yourself. Accept yourself as all that you are—with your human weaknesses and strengths, but also that you are a part of this great cosmic dream of that Cosmic Dreamer through which all existence is born. And through which we exist at this very moment! It is not a question of believing in a God of a particular kind, but of becoming conscious that one is more than one's name, one's mind, one's thoughts, and one's physical presence.

You are a product of Infinity, and therefore whatever you do can carry some meaning. You are significant because you are able to transfer energy not only at a material level through how you choose to act, but also through how you choose to feel, how you choose to relate to others.

So, good leaders are not spiritually fragmented in their approach. They are very integrated. They carry a vibration, a feeling, which conveys something that can have significance for other people. It is a question of giving direction to your energy, a positive direction. The more purpose-driven and creative direction you give your energy, the greater the creative energy-field you create around yourself. And leadership is nothing but the art of creating positive energy-fields, so that people and things are attracted into your life, into your sphere of energy and action.

CHAPTER-17

Inspiring Confidence
through Leadership

LESSON: Both, true self-confidence and the ability to inspire confidence within others, come from non-repression of the mystical aspect within you. And that mystical aspect is the naturally cheerful, joyful, playful, and spontaneous quality of being. This quality begins commanding the trust and confidence of people around you. Be natural and spontaneous. This is at the very heart of the true Vedantin.

A leader is, very simply put, somebody who inspires confidence. From the Vedantic and Hindu wisdom perspective, it is only the person who lives his or her own message with truth who truly gains the confidence of others. So this is what a leader needs to be aware about: it is not just what you say, but how you *are,* that is constantly sending a message to people. Positive leaders do not wear a façade. This can only come out of being grounded and centred in that which you seek to communicate. So it means that you have to act with heartfulness: real depth happens when people act out of that space which we call the spiritual heart. The more we become conscious and sensitive about acting spontaneously from the depths of ourselves, the more we find joy arising, and out of this joy comes real value and real virtue in that which we are doing. We become almost playful in our actions, and also intense.

A person in a good state of being starts having a Midas touch, and whoever comes in contact with such a person feels attracted to their leadership abilities. So be in a receptive mode, allow things to happen! When you do that, you have understood the deeper meaning of spontaneous action. Observe leaders' faces in everyday life: a lot of them have great stress and tension written on their faces, great anxiety and turmoil within because of their role and the pressures they have. But that is not the way of achieving a place of confidence. We must project peace. We must project trust. We must project doubtless confidence in our own ability. And through that comes the confidence of others. Know who you are—go to the very roots, and then you become clear and transparent to yourself. Out of this transparency, play your part as a leader. And suddenly you begin to see that your value in others' minds increases manifold.

The root of good action lies in awareness: the very realization that your consciousness can transform things itself becomes transformative! Take the challenge of being yourself *completely:* of functioning from your innermost core! You will then automatically give confidence to others. That is the meaning of what Krishna is constantly telling Arjun in the Bhagavad Gita. That if Arjun loses confidence in his own being by not acting spontaneously from his innermost core as a warrior, others too will lose confidence not only in him, but in themselves. He will stop being a positive role model, and that is disastrous not only for the individual himself, but for the whole unit and for society.

The power of the inner is said to be like a great, big tidal wave. But people are really afraid of being themselves: they want to continue being who they have been in the past. However, the secret of growth is to constantly look forward to new horizons; to go for things which are bigger than you, higher than you. That will inspire not only you, but others too. So drop the old patterns and work with a totally new spirit. Have respect for what you are. Only then will others have it too.

The Dharmasutras deal with the duties of a king,

and have great insights on leadership. The texts' ancient principles are still very relevant and sublime. They say in essence that a leader is to bring the quality of spirituality into his or her leadership role, but it is not about religion itself. Rather it's about a quality of being, which inspires confidence in others. And the thing to remember is that it is not about aggression. A lot of people think that being overly aggressive brings about confidence, but what it does is not allow you to take flight to your highest potential.

The mind of a good leader has a certain clarity about essential things: that you are not to waste your energy in things like aggression, but that instead you are to become so cool in your temperament, that being with you makes others feel the sense of coolness, this bliss of inner being. That is the most charismatic thing in existence. Let your energy become a compassion which touches others. A true leader is a builder of bridges. And when action arises out of building bridges between people, it leads to a harmonized energy of the entire team. That is essentially what every good leader should seek to do: harmonize individual energies to become one. To function as one. To flow as one.

Only a person who can relax his own tensions can seek to relax the tensions of others. And in so doing, automatically and spontaneously does confidence in each other arise. Religion and spirituality do not basically seem important when it comes to things like leadership. But a spiritual consciousness is important: it is not about our individual beliefs or disbeliefs, but about how we can create value and well-being in the moment. This is the essence of the matter. So make people feel unburdened of anxiety, by unburdening your own first!

The entire humanity has a collective unconscious. This is the finding of the great psychologist Carl Gustav Jung. Those people who can create a great sense of hope and well-being within this collective unconscious that humanity shares, go on to be the really influential leaders in a positive way (not a negative way). There are negative leaders who disturb this collective unconscious even more, and that leads to things like World Wars. We need to instead awaken and be more attentive to what Vedanta calls our original face, the pure self, for of it comes real and enduring confidence within ourselves, and within people we interact with.

CHAPTER-18

The Youthful and Strong Leader

LESSON: Vedanta implies feeling constantly connected to the timeless aspect of being. This makes you deeply relaxed and deeply energetic/strong, at the same time!

The secret of leadership energy is feeling youthful in spirit. Real youthfulness as defined by Vedanta and Hindu teachings is the feeling and understanding that you're not to be identified with the physical or mental circumference of your being, but rather with that timeless and ageless centre of your being which is ever-youthful, ever-energetic *(aujsik)*.

Real strength is the strength of the human spirit, and that is ageless. It is within you, deep within. And it is up to you: to be saturated with that spirit in all your leadership activities in the world. You will notice that there are some people who constantly radiate strength and energy to others. That is the real test of youthfulness. Youthfulness is the energy which shines out of a person and is transmitted to others. So it is a quality more than a particular thing. It is the ability to shine and radiate all that is good within you. From that aspect, everybody can remain and feel youthful. And in doing so you transcend all boundaries, and become a force of good for everybody because you have the capacity to radiate splendour and uplift others.

The aging process and the question of youthfulness, Indian philosophy says, is not a question of linear time. It is a question of transcending time, and functioning from that portion of your being within, which is free of the material and physical restrictions of time. That is what the whole mythological story of Yayati is supposed to connote: it is a parable that tells us how even the lengthiest physical life can be completely wasted if not used for spiritual realization, but instead used only to further one's physical lusts, material desires, and sensory enjoyments. King Yayati, a person of power and riches, acts most selfishly by bargaining with Death for an extension of his own life in exchange for those of his sons'. Yet his is an utterly wasted life by the end of it. The lesson is this: fulfilled living is not to be counted in years, but in the quality of spiritually realized moments we experience. Yayati stands as an example of a leader with misplaced priorities.

If you think in terms of youthfulness as a question of physical age, you are bound to be miserable. As you grow older, be free of the idea that you are caught up by the limitations of the body and mind. Freedom is the goal of all real religion, and the first thing is to decide to free yourself from the body-mind complex; to understand that your self-view and self-perception should not be coloured by it.

In all the mythologies of the world, there is the story of the elixir of life—that which allows us to never age. In all the Abrahamic religions, including Christianity, it features as the quest for the Holy Grail. In India it is the Amrit or elixir, for which both the *devas* and the *asuras* are fighting. In the legend of the Samudra Manthan, this parable is featured. In fact, the story is voiced all over Southeast Asian mythology. But really Amrit, that nectar, begins with understanding that our real body is not the one which is comprised of the physical elements alone, nor is it the one which is comprised of thoughts or the mental body. The real body of the human being is the *anandamayakosha*—the blissful body. It is the subtle body, which can experience the state of witness-ship. The physical body is called the *annamayakosha*, the vital body is called the *pranamayakosha* (because it is made of breath), the mental body is called *monomayakosha* because it comprises thoughts, *vigyanamayakosha* is the body of consciousness, and the ultimate body is that of Ananda or pure bliss: the *ananadamayakosha*. It arises and manifests spontaneously through your actions when you realize yourself to be timeless and ageless. With this ability to identify yourself as a timeless and ageless being, a new sort of spirituality is born in you. Your vision of life goes from being ordinary and mundane, to extraordinary. And when your vision of life itself becomes extraordinary, all that you touch becomes touched with the extraordinary.

The thing about great people in history is that their vision of life—their *darshana* or life philosophy—is touched by this higher vision of timelessness, of agelessness, of transcending the sense of local or circumstantial limitation. Which is why they become legendary—because their relevance is for all time. But it all begins with functioning at your most optimum, at what may be called the omega of your being (the summit of your being). And to function from the summit of your being is needed a recognition that the most essential part of you does not grow old. It is that part which can experience truth and bliss. It is that part which delights in working effortlessly; it is that part which is always in a state of non-tenseness, as the witness behind the activity which your mind and body are undertaking.

In Vedanta and Hindu spiritual philosophy, it is said

that each person has the capacity to keep giving birth to himself, even in this lifetime. In fact, the real Brahmin was called *dwija* or twice born: first there is a physical birth, but the second birth is a spiritual birth. So you can keep being reborn spiritually. You can keep renewing yourself at the level of spiritual energy. Each instant you can make a new spiritual beginning. This understanding and attitude brings a great deal of freedom, it brings a great sense of growth.

A lot of people stop growing simply because they do not understand that each instant can be an instant to evolve and grow. The willingness to grow, the willingness to evolve, is in fact what keeps one mentally and spiritually young. So that is the most important thing—the ability to not block ourselves at any stage of life, but to keep psychologically and spiritual evolving. Through inward spiritual evolution comes true youthfulness.

In finality, youthfulness requires a warmth of being from the heart of yourself. You should be constantly in a state of flowing, and not get stagnant. It's the capability of moving on with a sense of rejoicing, and not being stuck. This ability to flow unbounded, with a deep heartfelt love of life, is really what youthfulness is about. Through it, one develops a glow, a radiance that shines through within oneself and touches others in the process. And that is the most charismatic quality a leader can have— the quality of youthfulness.

CHAPTER-19

Everything Moves in Cycles

*LESSON: Flowing with change and with life's
universal cycles is the crux of Vedanta. It means
stepping back from over-reactivity, and calmly seeing
the larger picture. This creates maturity and relaxation
within your inner self, while deeply dynamizing your
outward actions! These are crucial attributes of great
leaders who have dealt effectively with change, and been
true value-creators for society and for planet Earth.*

Vedanta philosophy, much like other paths of
Indian mysticism, emphasizes that everything
moves in cycles. Whether it is the changing
seasons, whether it is the motion of the galaxies
and the planets: everything moves in an elliptical
or whirling circle of existence. In Buddhism, this

is characterized as the turning of the wheel. Everything is subject to this cycle. This understanding of cyclical change is extremely important when it comes to the understanding of Vedanta philosophy in the context of leadership. You see, one of the greatest things a leader has to deal with is constant change. So, by understanding the cyclic nature of existence itself, we are able to adjust ourselves to its flow.

The problem that happens with leadership is that people can become drunk on power. People can be overcome by what they have achieved. And then psychologically and spiritually they are not able to move in sync with the turning wheel of life. Then life will always be a disappointment, because they are not prepared for failures: they are only living for the peak experiences of life! The leader who lives only for peak experiences is not the best person to face a crisis situation or a catastrophe. A person must be able to function as calmly and efficiently during a downturn as they function during an upturn.

Indian mythology is replete with such examples of how to tide over both downturns and upturns of the wheel of life. We can look at the warrior prince Arjun: his life was a constant cycle of changing circumstances. As part of the Pandav brothers, he was deprived of his rights as a prince from his very childhood. Yet he continued excelling in his marksmanship, as an expert archer and went on to become a great warrior. Then again later in life, the brothers were sent into exile. Yet Arjun never shirked from being the best he could be. He came back to excel in the great Mahabharat war, and helped win the throne for his elder brother.

So too we can see in the ancient epic, the Ramayan, the very Vedantic and spiritual teaching about how Prince Ram did not lose his inner tranquillity in the midst of crisis. He was the favourite of the king, his father. He was the favourite of the people. He had all the qualities required to be a great leader. Yet due to very unfair circumstances, he was deprived of all that. But he never allowed those dire circumstances—even being sent into exile—affect his inner judgment of things or affect his enlightened state of being.

So it's the inner state which must remain unaffected by the cyclic motion of life, by the cyclic motion of circumstances. That is what makes a true leader of steel. That is what creates real strength when it comes to leadership ability. Otherwise, we may remain ordinary. And only a leader who allows himself to be transformed by the act of meditation, or by the act of contemplative inner silence and calmness, is one who is a true warrior in spirit. In a way this is part of the greater 'warrior code' of the leader.

To be a real winner in life, you must be able to move

with the cycle. When you can do that, you transcend the very cycle! The whole concept of liberation—*moksha* or 'nirvana'—in the Indian view of things is the ability to spiritually transcend the cycle of circumstance, to be liberated and free from its constant turning. It is descriptive of an inner state, of enlightened vision. We can only transcend our circumstances when inwardly we are so alert—as a witness to the cycle's functioning—that our consciousness has the power to go beyond it! Then only can we move out of our own projections and private imaginings, and go into the higher reality of existence. We are usually too loaded with ideas: the whole thing is to get rid of our prejudices, to go back to our fundamental roots. There lies the strength to transcend the cycle of circumstances.

Hence, this is a very mystical understanding: of how we are to actively and calmly take part in whatever life throws our way, in a manner where we can function not only as achievers but as meditators; as people who can function in sync with the mind of the cosmos itself. That is what realization means. That is what inner evolution means. A leader should be so evolved that he is never disturbed or frightened by the constant movement of the cycle of time. He's prepared, no matter what comes his way!

This is what it means to have a direct understanding of the innermost core of spiritual values for leadership.

It's all about our own consciousness coming face to face with that which is the best within us. Everything in life is interlinked: if we are in a leadership position, we have to realize that it is linked to our emotional state, to our psychological state, and most importantly to our spiritual state. So it becomes very important for the individual to address the spiritual or mystical state, if one is really to attain the higher potential of one's individual leadership ability.

Great leaders—and truly successful people—are those who can reconcile the spiritual part of their existence to the material responsibilities they have within the world. That is what spiritually conscious leadership and success mean.

CHAPTER-20

Total Action Comes through Surrender

LESSON: From the Vedantic angle, the only real devotion is surrender of the ego. This creates authenticity, self-power, and happiness for oneself, and within those one leads.

One of the most important things to understand when it comes to Vedanta philosophy are the concepts of total action and total surrender. It is said in Vedanta that total action only comes through the act of surrender *(samarpan)*. As long as the ego is not surrendered to the larger cosmic aspect, one's action is never total. And great leadership is all about holistic totality of action.

Therefore, it follows that for a person to be a great leader there needs to be a surrender of the ego. But that is not the only thing: what is really important is that one is warrior-like in one's vision, where one is ready to meet with death even, while on the field of battle or performing a dynamic action. One does not restrain one's highest self-nature in that state! That is what total action means, and such action is always rewarded. But it is not done for the reward! It is done for its own sake. It is done to express that which is hidden in you, as your inner depth of potentiality.

So what does it essentially take to be total in action? It needs us to first of all not be afraid of that essential human-ness, that essential vulnerability, which is within us. Bring not only your strengths into action, but bring all your different aspects of being. Holding nothing back. Be true to yourself. Very rare and few are those leaders who are so unafraid that they are willing to expose themselves completely. But remember, they are the only true leaders. They bring something of their heart into whatever they are doing. They are not worried about how people will judge them. They bring the holistic fullness of their feelings, their emotions, their logic, their rationality, their compassion into it. And fill their action with a oneness of energy, which is the sum total of all these!

This does not mean that one brings foolhardiness into what one is doing. It is important for one to be calm and sometimes restrained. The whole idea is that one is to be innocently joyful in one's energy, and not in a tension about being judged by others. When you are not in a tension of being judged by others, you can surrender your ego to what you are doing. Through that comes about a disappearance of psychological hindrances in the face of your work! Because essentially, only the truth of your own being liberates you. Only the realization of your self-truth and self-expression releases the energy to act dynamically.

Hence, don't be self-conscious! Be free from within. Don't be so mindful that people will see your real face: let them! It is immaterial. As it is, life is short. Don't be afraid to expose your real self, your real persona before others. That is the way of the mystic warrior. But leaders in the world are constantly self-conscious about their real personas: that is why very few leaders in history have actually been truly dynamic, truly spiritual in nature. In fact, the very idea of 'leadership' has put them into an artificial shell. But it in fact should be the opposite: a leadership position should put you in a position of strength. Where you realize that you are not the 'doer' of everything, but an instrument of the cosmos; that you have a great opportunity to express your true nature in your role as leader! And to take others in a flow towards self-fulfilment. But it all begins by transcending your own sense of self-consciousness and self-limitation.

Our ego is constantly shaped by the opinions of others. But we are to forget about the opinions of others in order to be total in action. Most of us have formed our self-opinions merely based on others' opinions, and that is the real tragic part of human life. Now, Krishna is very clear on this point to Arjun in the Bhagavad Gita: that it is no use being mentally shaped by what others think of you, so don't be afraid of being who you are! Don't be afraid of your own pure consciousness, the virgin spaces of your heart and mind. Because that is what will create totality in what you do. Else, you will live in dreams. You will be disturbed and shaped by somebody else's views. Realize the strength of your innermost being, and act through that! That is really the remembrance which is needed! Then automatically all you do will become more and more total. And becoming total, good results are bound to come.

A leader who can be open and total in action is always attractive for people. He is always a good team person, because people feel that he is not a hypocrite. Therefore, in order to be effective leaders, we are to shed all hypocrisy (which often accompanies leaders). Leaders can sometimes become hypocrites by not being aligned to the truth of their inner beings. Because of that, they are not able to bring the holistic totality of themselves into their actions. They often hold something back, trying to be too cautious perhaps, to show only what they want to show and conceal other aspects. But there is nothing to conceal eventually: life is a journey, but life is also a great pilgrimage to discover the temple of your own being. And in that temple exists the power of the universal and cosmic entity. Freely allow that power of the universal and cosmic entity to act through you. Absolutely freely! Through such a spirit of totally free action do you attain a very non-attached or detached way of functioning. And through this detached way of functioning, comes about a great force of value-based leadership ability and excellence.

CHAPTER-21

No Need to Be Faultless!

LESSON: Spirituality does not imply perfection but a pursuit of truth, consciousness, and bliss! Vedanta is never hypocritical: it reconnects us back to our spiritual roots without requiring us to act unnaturally or wear the mask of superiority. Genuinely great leaders consciously or unconsciously have this Vedantic attribute.

Vedanta teaches a very interesting thing: that life is not about being faultless, but is simply about knowing yourself spiritually! And knowing yourself, you come to see that so-called impeccable or faultless functioning is not needed. After all, we all have our own faults, our own weaknesses and shortcomings! But at the same time, we are comprised of sat-chit-ananda (truth-consciousness-bliss) in our inner beings. We are a part of the higher universal principle itself! Vedanta essentially teaches this aspect: that you're to realize that you are cosmic in your basic form and make-up. So there's nothing to worry about, nothing to blame yourself about even if you do make mistakes as a leader! Simply learn, repent, and improve! That is the way and the means to move forward boldly in your life and leadership roles.

This is a very important learning for leaders. We rarely spend enough time in knowing ourselves, in understating ourselves spiritually. This happens because we are often too caught up in feeling guilty about mistakes instead of looking forward, building on our strengths.

Vedanta says that the person who knows herself or himself in one's core of being automatically moves towards a higher realm of living. All that the person thinks thereafter, and acts upon thereafter, becomes more fulfilled and luminous. This feeling is liberating— it brings a great quality of dynamism with it. Through this great quality of dynamism, what one touches and endeavours to do becomes of great value.

So leadership begins with this very simple understanding: no need to be obsessive or afraid of being at fault or making mistakes. That only creates more fear of failure, more anguish. Yes, continue making the effort, continue applying yourself to the task, but don't be under the illusion that work perfection is your life's only goal. Our real life is our inner spiritual life. What is outside is only a reflection of it. Therefore, to live your life to the maximum, to live your life to the optimum as a leader and as an individual, it implies that you come to a situation where your mind realizes itself to be synonymous with the cosmic perfection. And once that starts happening, you are able to taste the true sense of joy which you may have been missing in your work, in your leadership roles, and so on.

Great leadership has to come from an inner quality of your being. If your inner quality of being is peaceful, your leadership too will be peaceful. If your inner quality of being is heavy and clouded with anguish, then you cannot expect your energy in the outer world to be optimistic and positive. Your energy too will get heavy, anguished in the same proportion. What we contemplate within ourselves spreads out as the work within our world! So put your energy not so much into perfecting things in the outer world, but put the completeness of your energy in finding the inherent perfection within yourself! Sometimes just leave the idea of outer achievement, leave the mind which wants to achieve, leave the ego which wants to perfect! And doing so itself is the meditative state. Doing so itself brings you to a position where you become decisive, where you become a great force for good in the world.

The biggest auto-hypnosis in the world is man having to believe that he is less than perfect. The attitude of Vedanta is that everything is already perfect. There is nothing to improve upon. Realizing that this divine joy of perfection exists within you, automatically creates a situation where you become a great creator of value and bliss within the world. The boundaries between you and your work dissolve: you come to a situation where the circle of your life does not keep revolving around the outer, but becomes about enriching the inner.

Make your leadership have the meditative quality of inner perfection. If it has that inner quality of perfection, then its outward manifestation will be successful, it will be fulfilling. It will always take people onto the right path. And it will always liberate you from your self-limitations. It will take the individual unto a merging with the universal element or the cosmic element. That is the real joy of life! You see, life is a situation where the real treasure is always missed, simply because we don't surrender the ego. The real treasure always exists in a place of egolessness. But for obsessive people, egolessness is a very far cry. They don't understand it; they are blind to it. And what does this do? This creates a certain blinkered vision in the world. Everything in nature is perfect. Rivers were perfect before we polluted them. The mountains were perfect before we littered them. The animals were perfect before we hunted them. The birds were perfect before we caged them. The stars and the planets are perfect till man reaches them. The person of Vedanta understands that there is perfection inherent in existence. It is only man's obsession with interfering in the processes of nature that leads to imperfection. Without man, everything exists in a natural state of perfection: this is the spiritual viewpoint. In the same way for our own work also: it is our own interference which sometimes leads to destructive things happening. Work should be creative, but because of man's ego—his lust for power, and so on—work often becomes destructive. Our actions in the world often become destructive. Our leadership potentiality often becomes destructive. And that is opposite to the Vedantic view of leadership success.

To make the journey of leadership so beautiful that you yourself feel happy and blissful from within, is the Vedanta leadership code. Through that is your inner gold and inner treasure perceived by yourself. That inner treasure is one of perfection, that inner gem is one of perfection!

Life's success is all about being deeply and truly responsive. Not out of past patterns, not out of what others are telling you, but out of realizing your inherent perfection! If you understand that, then whatever you do in the world will be full of consciousness; will be full of light; will be full of grace. The whole of your life will become an ecstasy. The whole of your work also will become an ecstasy. Why do people feel tired in their work? Why do they feel fatigued in their work? Why do they feel that their work is not so imbued with the beauty of higher energy? It's simply because they are not able to perceive their inner perfection. They're constantly agitated by the outer state of things. Inwardly, they are not relaxed. And you can only truly relax if you realize that beyond all calculation, beyond all logic, beyond the commercial view of life lies a situation where you can bring your most blissful and creative energy unto your tasks. If you do that, then automatically the material goals will get fulfilled, the creation of value will happen. And your interactions with people will also become greatly blissful. In other words, your relationships too will reach the highest rung. Most of our relationships are ordinarily on a very low rung. There may be a lot of resentment, there may be a lot of anger issues within relationships, there could be a constant see-saw between likes and dislikes, and so on. Our consciousness—when it comes to modern-day relationships—is not by and large healthy. This is reflected not only in our individual relationships, but in the relationships between nations, the relationships between religions, and so on. We are not able to relate fundamentally well to others, simply because the depths and vastness of ourselves have not been perceived by us, ourselves! The problem is, we look for perfection in others in a literal sense, and when that person does not meet our expectations, we feel let down! But remember the spiritual aspect always: within all beings is a common universal treasure that all of us have. Do not go by outward judgments on people: when you have the spiritual vision of looking at relationships, then they go smoothly, then they go beautifully. All the questions of prestige, money, power, and so on are replaced with a genuine respect between human beings. The motives become pure. Your self-bliss starts manifesting more into your life. You start feeling like you are divine. You start feeling like you're blissful. You start feeling like the essential core of your being is pulsating with the beauty of the entire cosmos. If you understand this aspect of Vedanta, you become a stronger and more capable person, of greater leadership value, within the world.

Why do misunderstandings happen between people? They happen mostly because people are constantly looking for perfection in the other person's situation, not realizing that this very obsession creates misunderstanding. Leave all this. This phenomenon of perfection has made people increasingly worried, anxious, suspicious of each other. On the one hand, we expect our friends to be perfect. On the other hand, the people we don't like, we discard as being absolutely worthless. But life is always in between: at an outward level we may have our differences, but at the inner level we are all part of the same consciousness. Yet we are constantly in conflict. Why? Often, because of institutions. The institution could be one of nation-states, could be one of race, could be one of religion. Man-made institutions often lead to friction and conflict between people! So the person who wants to be a good leader—who can make people go beyond conflict—looks at the spontaneous inner perfection within us as cosmic citizens, and not at the outward differences. If you look at outward differences, there will always be points of disagreement. We must look at the fundamental sameness of people! That resolves matters.

The problem is, there are so many ideologies in the world that they make us feel like we are all different: somebody insists that he is first and foremost a Muslim, a Christian, an Indian, an American and so on. These outward things have led to very negative leadership in the world. Relationships have been based on these outer labels, and these outer labels—by the very dint of their limited material utility—can never lead to peace. They only lead to more hypocrisy. They never lead to greater heights of being. They never lead to the religious quality of true nobility and courage. They always create divisions! And true leadership means dissolving boundaries, dissolving differences. That's where you become spontaneously capable of multidimensional evolution in every sphere: of mind, body, and spirit. This multidimensional evolution is what Vedanta is about. It's about integrating all the colours of the cosmic rainbow! And of realizing that at a fundamental level, we are all the same: at a fundamental level, we are part of the same eternal perfection.

Hence, through this very Vedantic quality of looking at things, we are able to change not only our own world, but are able to influence others in a better way. Because this attitude creates empathy. It makes us look at others with a compassionate eye. At the same time it creates a great self-respect within ourselves and also garners the respect of others. And having *respect for self plus others* is the very basis of great leadership. Without it, you are not honouring the larger life-energy which we are all born of and live within. The greater mind is one which is able to harness all of life's experience, and treat every moment like a chance to find ecstasy! That way, you reach towards being impeccable. Because in the end, only ecstasy, love, and bliss are near impeccable and faultless!

Acknowledgements

I wish to express my humble gratitude to the people who have made this series possible:

Anuj Bahri, my super literary agent at Red Ink.

Shikha Sabharwal and Gaurav Sabharwal, my wonderful publishers at Fingerprint! Publishing and their team.

Garima Shukla, my amazing and brilliant editor.

Family—my parents, partner Sohini, sister Priti, nieces, nephews, et al: you are my rock.

Gratitude also to my support team, friends, mentors, and well-wishers over the years.

Pranay is a mystic philosopher. He is an expert on Indian and world spirituality.

Pranay's modules on 'Advanced Spirituality for Leadership and Success' (PowerTalks/MysticTalks for public and corporate audiences) have won global acclaim.

Pranay is also a theatre personality and playwright. His original productions such as *From Kabir to Kavi* and *Soul Stir* have been acclaimed by world luminaries for their path-breaking spiritual content.

Pranay and his partner Sohini run the socio-cultural philanthropic commune TAS, whose initiatives such as 'Theatre Against Drugs' (for addicts), 'Geetimalya' (for underprivileged children) and 'Shohaag' (for women empowerment) are well-known and have become movements.

Presently, Pranay is collating his discourses on mind-body-spirit themes for various book series.

Connect with him on his website: pranay.org